SPELLING
A Teacher's Survival Kit

Sue Palmer

Acknowledgements

The author would like to thank all those teachers and pupils who have contributed ideas for this book and/or trialled material and ideas; Gordon Jarvie, who started it off, and Janet Weller and Stephen Attmore, who finished it.

We are grateful to Penguin Books Limited for permission to reproduce the poem 'Spelling Rules, OK?' from *The Jungle Sale* by June Crebbin, (Viking Kestrel, 1988) © June Crebbin, 1988.

Designed and illustrated by Jake Tebbit, Toft, Cambridge.

Oliver & Boyd
Longman House
Burnt Mill
Harlow
Essex CM20 2JE

An imprint of Longman Group UK Ltd

First published 1991
Second impression 1992
ISBN 0 05 004494 X
Set in New Century Schoolbook 10/14pt

Produced by Longman Singapore Publishers Pte Ltd
Printed in Singapore

The publisher's policy is to use paper manufactured from sustainable forests.

How to use this book

The National Curriculum Guidelines for England and Wales require that spelling should be taught to all children, throughout their primary years and well into the secondary school. The Guidelines also require, in their Programmes of Study, that spelling should be dealt with 'within the context of [children's] own reading and written work'. In Scotland, similar requirements for the teaching of spelling are set out in *English Language 5–14*.

This book is intended to give teachers the background knowledge about spelling and practical advice on classroom techniques which will enable them to fulfil these requirements, making the teaching of spelling a simple and natural part of everyday classroom practice.

The book may be used like a manual. Each of its five sections is designed to be self-explanatory, with cross-referencing where necessary. Teachers are advised to read the first and second sections for an overview of theory and practice, but otherwise the material may be 'dipped into' as required.

It is possible to spell a word correctly by chance, or because someone prompts you, but you are a scholar only if you spell it correctly because you know how.

Aristotle

Spelling Rules, OK?

Each Monday we're given ten spellings
To learn by the end of the week,
And some are easy like 'lovely',
 And some are hard like 'unique'.

There's a lot of rules to remember,
Like when to change y into i
As in jellies and wellies and berries,
And when you want more than one fly ...

You change f into v to make half into halves,
There's a piece of pie in piece,
There's i before e except after c
As in thief and in chief and in niece ...

To make stare into staring, you knock off the e,
There's a silent k in knot,
To make skip into skipping, you double the p –
It's hard to remember the lot.

But by the end of the week, I'm word-perfect,
And then, what I really detest
Is when the teacher is busy
And *forgets* the spelling test!

And if, on the following Monday,
I manage to get them all right,
My teacher then says, 'But the real test
Is how well you spell when you write!'

Jane Crebbin

Contents

Section 1: *A Question of Spelling*

> How important is spelling?

The subject of spelling can arouse fierce passions in educational circles. On one side, some teachers argue that it is of little importance, and that emphasis on correct spelling detracts pupils' attention from the real matter in hand – that is, learning to write clearly and cogently. On the other side, teachers (and often parents) contend that correct spelling is an important facet of written work, indicating the writer's control of the English language and consideration for his/her reader. Debate therefore rages as to whether teachers should direct their attention to the 'deep' or 'surface features' of language when developing their pupils' writing skills.

My freind is an elifant he lets me rid on is bak and he sqirts warter at my enememys with is trunck. his feat get mudy somtimes and mum hats him comeing in the howse she keps tacking him for warks and trieing to loose him.

Lovely story!

My freind is an elephant he lets me ride on is bak and he sqirts wafter at my enemies with his trunk. His feat get mudy somtimes and mum hats him comeing in the house. She keps tafking him for wafks and trieing to lose him.

Watch your spelling. Correct each word 3 times.

As is usual in such debates, there are important points to be considered on both sides. In the example on page 3, most teachers would first of all be anxious to respond to the gentle humour and insight shown in the child's work. They might wish to suggest a few minor changes to the composition, to improve the cohesion and flow of the writing (e.g. changing 'and' to 'so' in line 6), or point out ways in which punctuation could enhance its clarity. They would almost certainly wish to encourage the child to expand on this elegant little piece of fantasy, thus perhaps developing his or her obvious pleasure in creative writing.

Anything more than the most cursory attention to spelling in this first response would probably be counter-productive to the writer's further progress. But the teacher might nevertheless note the types of spelling errors the child is making, with a view to helping him/her improve the surface features of work in the future. The teacher might wish to point out one or two spellings which the child could correct in the redrafting of the piece, and to which attention at this particular point in his/her development could pay dividends. Also, the teacher might wish to ensure that the 'spelling curriculum' of the classroom helps all children improve their spelling painlessly, so that spelling is no handicap to fluency in their day-to-day writing.

Some children who are insecure about spelling become reluctant to write. Others write volubly but find that their readers have difficulty understanding their work. And, of course, people in the world outside school value correct spelling and often equate it (wrongly) with intelligence and aptitude with language. We therefore owe it to our pupils to ensure that they can spell as well as possible.

Yes, It's very good. But what does 'Praticle mins' mean?

Is spelling caught or taught?

The debate about spelling may be further confused by the issue of whether the ability to spell is 'caught' or 'taught'. Some would argue that teaching is not in fact necessary – that children can learn to spell naturally, through meeting correct spellings in their reading and through being allowed to experiment with spelling in their own writing. Those who espouse this theory sometimes argue that spelling instruction is actually harmful, in that it interferes with children's natural development.

On the other hand, those on the side of teaching spelling point to the large number of poor spellers who have patently failed to learn 'naturally', and to the many irregularities in the English language which make the learning of spelling difficult. They contend that teaching of spelling is essential.

Again, there is no reason why we cannot take the best from both sides of the argument. Research with young children has indicated that, when allowed to experiment with their own 'invented spelling', many of them do develop much implicit understanding of the spelling system. It seems wise, therefore, to give children the opportunity to 'catch' spelling in this way in the early stages of literacy, and as long as 'invented spellings' are not detracting from their own and other people's understanding of their work.

But the vast majority of children eventually require structured help to become proficient at spelling, and a significant minority require a great deal of help to make progress beyond the most elementary stage. The school must therefore be ready to provide well-structured teaching support at the appropriate times to help all children attain their full potential in this area. The form that teaching support should take is best decided by looking at the ways in which people process the spellings of words.

How do people remember spelling?

There are four main ways in which people process the spelling of words.

Visual
'Does it look right?'
Writer responds to the shapes of words and the patterns of letter-strings within words.

Auditory
'Sound it out!'
Writer recognises the relationship between sounds and letters or groups of letters, and analyses words in these terms.

Linguistic
'Why is it spelt like that?'
Writer is aware of relationships between words or parts of words, based on meaning, syntax, derivations, etc.

Kinesthetic
'Let the spelling come out of the end of your pencil!'
Spelling as a grapho-motor skill: writer is accustomed to making specific hand-movements to produce particular words or letter-strings.

Adults who are proficient at spelling use a mixture of these processing skills when they are writing, though the balance of the mixture seems to vary from person to person. Recent research by Margaret Peters *et al* suggests strongly that the majority of good spellers rely heavily on the *visual processing of spelling*. It therefore follows that teachers should attempt to develop visual strategies in their pupils, as far as possible.

It cannot be denied, however, that some understanding of the sound/symbol relationships in the English language is necessary to spelling competence, and some adults with poor visual memories appear to lean very heavily on *auditory processing* of words. This suggests that pupils will benefit from the development of auditory strategies (perhaps especially the breaking up of words into syllables for ease of processing and sensitisation to medial vowel-sounds in syllables e.g. 'măth-ĕ-măt-ĭcs').

Kinesthetic processing of spelling is common in frequently-used words and letter-strings (and can sometimes cause misspellings, as when a writer produces 'withe' for 'with', adding an 'e' as is expected in 'the' and many other words). This processing strategy will, of course, develop as a result of attention to spelling alongside the teaching of handwriting, and the extent to which pupils have opportunities to write and thus practise their spelling.

Linguistic processing strategies are obviously used most frequently by those spellers whose awareness of the English language has been most fully developed: hence, in general, good spelling goes with overall proficiency in literacy skills. The emphasis on language knowledge which is called for by the National Curriculum should ensure that more pupils develop a strength in this area. Learning about spelling should be linked wherever possible to learning about the English language in general – its vocabulary, usage, grammar and history.

Teaching methods should, of course, help pupils to develop all the methods of processing mentioned above so that they may use whichever is most appropriate to their own mental make-up. However, there are inevitably fashions in educational methods, and there is often more emphasis placed on one type of processing than another. In recent years, the work of Peters *et al* has unfortunately been synthesised in some quarters into the single phrase 'spelling is a visual skill'. This has resulted in some lopsided teaching approaches, which have been entirely unsuitable for many children.

Teachers are urged to remember that human beings are all different, and different people will process spelling in different ways!

Who cares about spelling? Milton spelt *dog* with two *g*'s. The American Milton, when he comes, may spell it with three, while all the world wonders, if he is so minded.

Augustine Birrell

Are there developmental stages in spelling skill?

Some researchers claim to have identified developmental stages common to all children in the acquisition of spelling skills. The chart below shows some basic features in one developmental model:

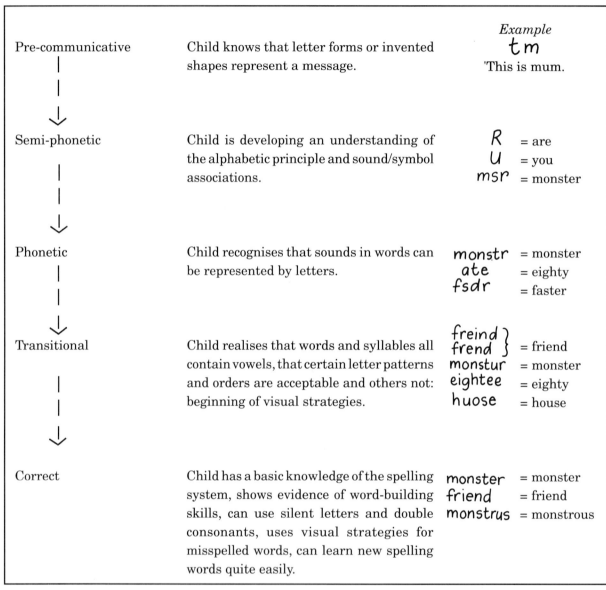

		Example
Pre-communicative	Child knows that letter forms or invented shapes represent a message.	t m 'This is mum.
Semi-phonetic	Child is developing an understanding of the alphabetic principle and sound/symbol associations.	R = are U = you msr = monster
Phonetic	Child recognises that sounds in words can be represented by letters.	monstr = monster ate = eighty fsdr = faster
Transitional	Child realises that words and syllables all contain vowels, that certain letter patterns and orders are acceptable and others not: beginning of visual strategies.	freind } frend } = friend monstur = monster eightee = eighty huose = house
Correct	Child has a basic knowledge of the spelling system, shows evidence of word-building skills, can use silent letters and double consonants, uses visual strategies for misspelled words, can learn new spelling words quite easily.	monster = monster friend = friend monstrus = monstrous

adapted from *Bright Ideas: Spelling* by Bentley and Karavis

The 'transitional' stage in this model roughly correlates with Level 2 of the National Curriculum Spelling Attainment Target, which for the average pupil is reached around the end of Key Stage 1 (in Scotland: level A6).

Most supporters of a developmental model would argue that, until children have reached the 'transitional' stage, classroom emphasis on correctness in spelling is likely to be ineffective, and may even be counter-productive. It may make children anxious about spelling correctness, rendering them less keen to write, and thus denying them sufficient opportunities to produce the 'experimental spellings' which will develop their awareness.

While the developmental model has yet to be proved, these arguments seem sufficiently cogent to be taken into account in the selection of teaching methods during Key Stage 1. While every effort should be made to help children develop awareness of the elements necessary for good spelling – in order to fulfill the terms of the National Curriculum – this should be pursued as far as possible without making a fetish of 'correctness' in their own emergent writing. (See Section 2.1, page 11.)

The spelling of words is subordinate. Morbidness for nice spelling and tenacity for or against some one letter or so means dandyism and impotence in literature.

Walt Whitman

Orthography is so absolutely necessary for a man of letters, or a gentleman, that one false spelling may fix a ridicule upon him for the rest of his life; and I know a man of quality who never recovered from the ridicule of having spelled *wholesome* without the *w*.

Lord Chesterfield

Are some children just bad spellers?

There are many reasons for poor spelling. Before leaping to the conclusion that a pupil is simply a 'bad speller', the teacher should, of course, look for possible physical or emotional problems which might be at the root of the problem. Children with poor eyesight, hearing difficulties or poor hand–eye coordination can obviously encounter problems in learning to spell. Emotional difficulties can interfere with a pupil's learning in many ways, but anxiety seems to have a particularly notable effect on spelling.

Teachers might also examine the way a child has been taught, and try to determine whether the methods employed have been unsuitable for his/her preferred learning methods. A different approach might help the child achieve a greater degree of success.

However, there certainly seems to be a minority of children who have more difficulty with spelling than others, as a result of a specific learning difficulty. Their inexplicable spelling problems can be a source of distress for such pupils – people often equate poor spelling with low intelligence or lack of effort. In fact, poor spelling is not an indicator of low intelligence (many highly intelligent people – like Einstein, Hans Christian Andersen and Leonardo da Vinci – have been poor spellers), and children with a specific difficulty in this area often try harder than their peers, with little success. Repeated failures in spelling can cause them to become despondent and lose interest in written work; it can even lead to behavioural problems.

Such children can often be helped to improve their spelling considerably, particularly if the teacher is able to assess the underlying reasons for the spelling difficulties. Section 4 of this manual gives some suggestions for diagnostic assessment of spelling problems and pointers to methods of remediation.

They spell it Vinci and pronounce it Vinchy; foreigners always spell better than they pronounce.

Mark Twain

Section 2 *Spelling and the National Curriculum*

in Scotland: Language 5–14 Curriculum Policy

Key Stage 1 – Infants
Scotland: Levels A & B

2.1

Teaching spelling or developing writing?
There are two main problems facing teachers at Key Stage 1 with regard to spelling.

- How does one reconcile *teaching* spelling with the theory that spelling competence is a developmental process (see Section 1.4), and the related theory that children require to develop an appreciation of patterns through their own 'experimental spelling'?

- Secondly, if an emphasis is placed on spelling, children may become preoccupied with 'correctness' in their writing at the expense of quality and quantity of output. They may limit their choice of vocabulary to 'safe' words and phrases that they know how to spell, and resort to formula-writing of the 'Yesterday I went to the shops' variety. Fearful of making mistakes, they may also become less willing to write at any length, thus impeding their development as writers as well as ensuring fewer opportunities for the 'experimental spelling' mentioned above.

It seems possible that by teaching spelling within the context of children's own written work the teacher may actually inhibit spelling development rather than promote it.

Spelling and children's own written work
We recommend therefore that there should be as little emphasis on spelling as possible as far as children's own writing is concerned. When pupils are required to compose stories, accounts, reports, etc. of their own, attention should be focused on the effectiveness of the writing – expression, clarity, structure and so on – not on the correctness of the spelling.

Praise should be given where words are spelled correctly or almost correctly, and where pupils have attempted the spelling of new, unusual, or difficult words; less successful spellings may be glossed over and criticism of spelling avoided whenever possible. Children who ask 'How do you spell ...?' during the course of a piece of writing can be encouraged to 'Have a go' rather than referred immediately to word books or dictionaries (consulting which anyway interrupts the flow of a child's writing). Some teachers suggest the use of a 'magic line' for unknown portions of a word – children write the initial and any other known letters and put a line where the unknown letters would go.

The teaching of spelling should be covered elsewhere in the curriculum, on occasions where pupils are not simultaneously concerned with the questions of composition and conveying meaning through their writing. We suggest that spelling can be successfully taught through the media of:

a) handwriting, and
b) the teaching of phonics for reading.

Spelling and phonics

The question of phonics teaching raises another long-term controversy. For many years now, trends in the teaching of reading at Key Stage 1 have been based on a 'meaning-driven model' of the reading process. Thus teachers have tried to develop children's reading ability, as far as possible, through meaningful reading experiences (just as writing is developed through meaningful writing experiences). Such terms as the language experience approach, real books and apprenticeship reading are associated with these methods. The National Curriculum Guidelines (and Curriculum Policy for Scotland) assume that these methods are now in general use.

Phonics teaching, with its emphasis on a specific reading skill, has sometimes been seen as inconsistent with a meaning-driven model of reading. However, most teachers have been reluctant to abandon teaching about phonics; and research (e.g. Bryant and Bradley) has continued to suggest that phonological awareness is an important element in the development of literacy. The National Curriculum also requires that, by Level 2, children should have begun to use phonic cues to tackle unknown words. In 1991 the English HMI Report The Teaching and Learning of Reading in Primary Schools made it clear that successful schools managed to balance meaningful reading activities with some instruction in phonics.

The obvious way to achieve such a balance would seem to be the teaching of phonics away from meaningful reading situations. Thus, when reading for meaning, children's attention is concentrated on meaning. At other times, and through other enjoyable classroom activities, their awareness of sound-symbol associations is being gradually developed. This awareness is then available to them when they read.

Teaching material for phonics abounds. The Letterland material (developed by Lyn Wendon) has proved very popular with children and teachers alike over recent years. Letterlinks (Jessie Reid and Margaret Donaldson) is another highly structured programme which can be followed alongside, but apart from, meaningful reading activities.

The same basic information about phonics which is helpful for reading at this stage is at the basis of the early spelling instruction required by the National Curriculum. If children are following a structured phonic course, they will develop their awareness of basic sound-symbol associations and letter patterns. Just as this awareness will gradually become available to them in their reading, it should also come to underlie their experimentation with spelling.

Handwriting and spelling

The careful and thorough teaching of handwriting is extremely important if pupils are to develop fluent writing skills at a later date, and this is acknowledged in the National Curriculum Attainment Target 5 (Scottish Writing Attainment Target 5). Handwriting lessons can also incorporate important information about spelling.

First of all, children can reinforce basic letter sounds as they learn to form the letters correctly (again Wendon's *Letterland* material can be useful here).

Later, handwriting practice can focus attention on the most commonly-used words in children's writing. This is the opportunity for pupils to practise the writing and spelling of such words as *the, there, they, them, then* or *see, saw, say, said* – which they use often in their own written work (see list of commonly-used words in Section 4.2). Handwriting practice can also reinforce simple spelling patterns (e.g. *feet, street, meet*). As pointed out in Section 1.3, spelling is partly a kinesthetic skill, and repeated practice of a particular group of letters to refine handwriting should aid the learning of that word or spelling pattern.

See also Section 2.4 – Wordbooks, dictionaries and spelling checkers.

My spelling is Wobbly. It's good spelling but it wobbles and letters get in the wrong places.
'Winnie-the-Pooh'

By the time the average child reaches Key Stage 2 (around 7.5–8 years), he/she should have reached the 'transitional' stage of spelling development (see Section 1.4) – the stage when specific teaching about spelling should be beneficial. Henceforth, there are two main ways in which teaching about spelling can be approached:

- on-going, 'incidental' teaching when a spelling word or rule crops up for an individual or group;

- systematic spelling instruction.

The programme of study for Key Stage 2 clearly supports an 'incidental approach', adding the words 'in the context of their own writing and reading' to each of the two paragraphs specifically related to spelling. Most teachers would probably agree that, ideally, this is the more congenial of the two teaching methods. Pupils who can pick up spelling rules and patterns as they go along, as an integral feature of their developing writing skills, are most likely to turn into 'natural' spellers. We give below and in Section 3 some ideas and strategies for ensuring that incidental learning of spelling becomes a routine feature of classroom life.

However, the statements of attainment for Spelling in Key Stage 2 involve many more spelling points than those mentioned in the programme of study and, in a busy classroom, it may prove impossible to ensure that all pupils receive all the help and direction they require within the context of their own writing and reading. Furthermore, many teachers feel that they are not themselves sufficiently confident about spelling patterns and rules to ensure that they cover them adequately on an incidental basis. Some schools may wish therefore to supplement their incidental teaching with the occasional structured spelling course. Comments and recommendations regarding such a systematic approach are given at the end of this section.

Whatever approach is adopted, it is important to remember that spelling competence is only one minor facet of literacy, and there are many other areas of writing skill which the teacher must encourage. Spelling should never be accorded such undue importance that pupils are discouraged from writing for fear of making spelling errors. And sometimes it will be necessary to ignore spelling altogether, when concentrating on some other aspect of writing.

Incidental teaching: 'in the context of their own writing and reading'

For incidental teaching to be successful, the teacher must have clearly defined methods by which they and the class will proceed. Such methods should ideally become a routine part of class activities.

1 The first essential is that pupils should have a **strategy for learning the spelling of words** which they need to know. Such a strategy, which involves the use of 'eye, ear, hand and brain', is given in Section 3

(Spelling: Advice to pupils 1). This page may be photocopied for distribution to pupils, so that the strategy may be taught and discussed, and then the sheet retained for reference. It requires frequent revision in the early stages, so that the strategy becomes habitual, and any spelling activities carried out in the classroom should conform to it.

2   Pupils require a routine **system for dealing with spelling queries** which arise during their day-to-day writing activities (see Section 3.4 and Spelling: Advice to pupils 2). Such a system should minimise the importance of spelling during the process of composition, make access to correct spelling (when the time is right) as simple as possible, and involve the pupil in *learning* the spelling, rather than merely copying it down. Sheet 2 is also in the form of a pupils' guide, intended for photocopying, distribution and discussion. The pupils can then retain their sheets as *aide memoires* until the system becomes automatic.

3   A further essential for the incidental teaching of spelling is a well-structured and simple **system for the marking of work**, helping pupils to recognise which words they are spelling wrongly. This should be backed up by a routine for **spelling corrections**, which will involve pupils in *learning* the spellings rather than merely copying them. (Spelling: Advice to pupils 3, is a photocopiable worksheet for pupils, and Section 3.5 gives teacher's notes on this marking policy.)

4   It will also be helpful if there is the opportunity for practice and reinforcement of the spellings which pupils have needed to learn over the course of a few weeks. A method of **individual assessment** is given in Section 3.6 (with Spelling: Advice to pupils 4 – a photocopiable worksheet for pupils), which should help ensure that each pupil learns and practises the words which he or she finds particularly tricky.

5   The National Curriculum programme of study also requires that pupils should be encouraged and shown how to **check spellings in a dictionary**. Photocopiable worksheets to familiarise pupils with the use of a dictionary are provided (Spelling: Advice to pupils 5a and 5b), but on the whole we recommend that pupils in the lower junior stage should consult the teacher rather than the dictionary wherever possible. Until one has achieved a reasonable degree of spelling competence, consulting a dictionary can be a time-consuming and frustrating activity – many children simply give up trying and thus do not increase their spelling vocabulary. As children become more proficient spellers, they can be directed to the dictionary as the teacher feels appropriate (see Section 2.4).

6   Teachers should also take opportunities to alert pupils to **facets of spelling which are highlighted by their work in other curriculum areas**. During projects in science, history, geography, etc., there will be occasions when attention can naturally be drawn to relevant word-families,

prefixes and word derivations (see Section 3.8, for teacher's notes on Project Spelling Banks).

7   Finally, there are certain spelling errors which crop up repeatedly in children's work, and which individual pupils require help and practice to eradicate. Particularly significant are confusions of homophones (e.g. *there/their*), and difficulties with doubling/dropping of final *e* and changing of *y* to *i*. In Section 5 of this book we provide a number of photocopiable worksheets covering the most common of these **'spelling sticking points'**. These can be given, as and when the occasion arises, to children whose written work demonstrates that they are having difficulty with a particular point. Most children will need further reinforcement of the point at a later date, perhaps through computer games or other spelling activities.

It may take some time to teach all these routines and strategies and integrate them into day-to-day classroom practice. Once they are established, however, they take up very little of the teacher's and the pupils' time, and they ensure that pupils are actively *learning* to spell as they go about their everyday activities across the curriculum.

Systematic teaching of spelling

Learning is largely concerned with the patterning of information in the brain – our understanding of a subject develops as we gradually build up an increasingly complex pattern of concepts and knowledge. The human brain appears to carry out the patterning process naturally, and it is through this active mental processing of information that children gradually develop spelling competence. By giving 'incidental' help with spelling, when pupils specifically require it in the context of their own writing, the teacher helps to facilitate and direct the natural process of patterning.

However, it cannot be denied that some children seem to develop an appreciation of spelling more readily than others: their minds seem more

adept at patterning this particular sort of information. At the same time, some teachers are more knowledgeable about spelling than others, and better able to intervene at the most appropriate moment with the most appropriate information – expanding upon a spelling point or rule when a pupil asks about a word, for instance, or identifying relevant groups of words to add to a project spelling bank.

For those pupils and teachers who are less naturally spelling-orientated, it may be helpful to supplement the incidental teaching methods described above with some systematic teaching of spelling. Despite the unfashionability of 'decontextualised' teaching methods, it seems likely that systematic study of a rule-based topic such as spelling will aid the development of intellectual patterning. A short course in spelling (covering, say, one term per school year) should be helpful in establishing ground-rules about the topic – the 'background patterns' against which incidental learning can take place.

The teaching materials adopted for a structured course should be suited as far as possible to the needs and abilities of the pupils concerned (e.g. dealing with words which the pupils actually use and need, rather than long lists of similarly-spelled but often obscure words), and might be linked to other connected areas of study, such as handwriting or knowledge about language.

The author's series of four books, *Mind Your Spelling*, was devised to be used in this way in the junior years. Each book in the series provides a systematic spelling course based on those learning strategies most appropriate to the age group, and covering the words with which pupils are most likely to need extra help. The two 'Monster' books for lower juniors link spelling to the development of a fluent handwriting style. The 'S.P.E.L.L.' books for upper juniors and lower secondary classes link it to the pupils' growing awareness of language and grammatical usage.

I don't see any use in spelling a word right, and never did. I mean, I don't see any use in having a uniform and arbitrary way of spelling words. We might as well make all our clothes look alike and cook all our dishes alike.

Mark Twain

Many pupils in the early stage of secondary school still require a fair amount of help with spelling, and the suggestions given in Section 2.2 for 'incidental' and/or 'structured' teaching methods should be of help to teachers at Key Stage 3 (Scottish Levels C & D). IT IS RECOMMENDED THAT SECTION 2.2 SHOULD BE CONSULTED BEFORE READING FURTHER.

'Within the context of their own writing and reading'

The routines and strategies necessary for 'incidental' teaching of spelling (see Section 2.2, pages 14–16) in the secondary school should be taught and developed by the pupils' English teacher but, to be most effective, they should then be employed across the curriculum by all subject specialists. It will, of course, be the responsibility of the English Department to ensure that other staff know their own part in spelling routines. A short checklist of the information other subject specialists need is given at the end of this section (page 19).

experiment   evidence
apparatus   economic
filtration   social
solution   industrial
              agriculture

mathematics   - ology
arithmetic   - graph -
parallel   geo

The context of pupils' own writing and reading widens very considerably upon entry to the secondary school. The introduction of specialist subject areas exposes them to an ever-widening range of specialised vocabulary. Many spelling problems, especially in the first couple of years, are the result of pupils' uncertainty with this new vocabulary. It can be very helpful, therefore, if the words they are encountering in various subject areas can be isolated from the subject study and discussed *as words* within the English class. Suggestions for help with **spelling of specialised vocabulary** are given in Section 3.9, but the activity should obviously involve discussion of *meaning* as well. Again, this strategy involves the English specialist seeking the cooperation of colleagues in other subject areas.

Systematic teaching of spelling

If a 'structured' course is required, the author's 'S.P.E.L.L.' series (*Mind Your Spelling, Books 3* and *4*) is appropriate in interest-level to the early secondary years and fulfils the requirements of the National Curriculum for spelling attainment at Levels 4, 5 and 6 (in Scotland, Levels D, E and onwards). It also relates spelling to other areas of knowledge about language; e.g. inflectional endings on verb forms and plural nouns; common nominal, adjectival and adverbial suffixes; word derivations and spellings of words with related meanings.

Teachers will also find the publication *Words Alive* by Bob Monaghan and Sue Palmer helpful for word study at Levels 6 and 7. Its photocopiable worksheets cover many interesting aspects of etymology and morphemology, again integrating opportunities for spelling instruction with the development of knowledge about language.

First aid

A further responsibility of the English teacher in the secondary school is to provide first aid for those few pupils who are still, in spite of everything, 'just bad spellers' (see Section 1.5). Section 4 of this book offers suggestions for helping such pupils overcome their handicap.

CHECKLIST OF POINTS TO BE COVERED WITH OTHER SUBJECT SPECIALISTS

1   Learning strategy for new words: LOOK and THINK
                                        SAY and LISTEN
                                        COVER, WRITE and CHECK

2   When asked how to spell a word:
        Write it down, ask the pupil to employ the strategy above.
        Don't spell it out, don't let the pupil merely copy it.

3   Corrections. Choose up to four wrongly-spelled words from a single piece of work, and write the correct spellings at the end. Expect pupils to use the above learning strategy and write correct spellings on the back page of the book (Spelling Page). Check these (or have them checked) occasionally.

4   If possible, provide lists of the words on each pupil's Spelling Page at regular intervals, for individual testing by the English teacher. Or, alternatively, arrange individual testing yourself.

5   If possible, provide lists of prospective specialised vocabulary on a termly basis, for use in English lessons.

The National Curriculum guidelines make frequent references to the use of wordbooks (collections of commonly used words, compiled either for individual children or for the whole class), dictionaries and computer spelling checkers. The guidelines suggest that pupils should be able to use these to look up spellings for themselves and to check spellings when editing their work.

Wordbooks

Some children in Key Stage 1 like to have access to a collection of words they commonly use, and a word book compiled for the individual (or a class word bank or word poster) is a means of providing this. It can also provide practice of alphabetical order, knowledge of which is necessary in many contexts.

However, it has already been argued in Section 2.1 (pages 11 – 13) that an overemphasis on 'correctness' in infants' written work is likely to be counter-productive in the long run. When compiling word books, either for individual children or for class use, teachers should try to ensure that they are used in a positive way, not as a source of inhibition.

Dictionaries

Pupils should be introduced to simple picture dictionaries in the earliest stages of primary school, and encouraged to use dictionaries and develop reference skills throughout their education. They should, of course, be used as a source of information on the meaning and, later, the etymology and structure of words. They are also the most obvious means of introducing alphabetically-arranged reference material, which will have many further applications as time goes on. A wide range of dictionaries is now available, with different ones suitable to different developmental levels.

However, as a spelling aid dictionaries are usually of limited usefulness to inexpert spellers:

- looking up words can be an extremely time-consuming occupation;

- the less able speller may have difficulty in locating words (how, for instance, could one guess where to look for *know, write, early, many,* or *once?*)

If constantly referred to a dictionary for spelling words, some pupils become frustrated and lose confidence in themselves as spellers, some may spend more time ploughing through the dictionary than they spend actually writing, some may simply cease bothering to look words up at all.

Until pupils have developed a reasonable degree of spelling competence, therefore, the teacher may prefer to provide spellings (see Section 3 – pages 22 – 25) for day-to-day writing tasks. Pupils should be taught how to use a dictionary to find the meaning of a word, and for the checking of spellings when no adult is at hand. (Worksheets on dictionary skills are provided in Section 3.) Teachers should also take the opportunity to use the dictionary alongside pupils whenever they themselves are doubtful of the spelling of a word.

Practice of this kind should ensure that dictionary skills are developed. As spelling competence develops, pupils' reliance on the dictionary can be gradually increased, and their dependence on the teacher as a source of correct spelling reduced (this is not expected until Level 5 in the Attainment Targets – late junior or early secondary level).*

Computer spelling checkers

Spelling checkers are now available for most word-processing packages, and pupils should have the opportunity of using them from Key Stage 2 onwards. They are, however, as their name suggests, merely *checkers*, not *teachers* of spelling. They are very efficient at picking up the most common spelling mistakes (e.g. *frend* for *friend*), or those which are due to typing errors, but most school computers do not have the memory capacity for an extensive lexicon. There can, therefore, be significant difficulties in their use for younger pupils or poor spellers:

1) only the most sophisticated spelling checkers (using powerful computers) can make any attempt to distinguish between homophones, such as *their / there* or *practise / practice*, which are very common in English;

2) generally, spelling checkers have been devised for commercial use and the vocabulary with which they deal is not always appropriate to the needs of younger pupils or poor spellers (watch out for those of American origin!);

3) when a spelling checker identifies a misspelling, it can usually provide alternatives only on the basis of the first few letters – thus a misspelling like *yousless* (for *useless*) may summon up a useless list of suggested words, such as *you, young, youth* and *youthful*;

4) spelling checkers provided for an American market may provide American rather than English versions of common words (e.g. *color, center*);

5) the checking of a long passage with a large number of errors can be time-consuming for the novice.

While pupils usually enjoy the novelty of using a spelling checker for a time, it can, like the dictionary, become a frustrating and counter-productive activity. Apart from practice and group sessions with younger pupils, it is best used by proficient spellers as an aid to the editing of their work, particularly for the identification of typing errors.

* Pupils whose spelling remains weak may find a spelling dictionary helpful at this stage, e.g. *The Pergamon Dictionary of Perfect Spelling* by Christine Maxwell (E.J. Arnold).

To make dictionaries is dull work.

Dr Samuel Johnson

Section 3: *Spelling Routines and Strategies Across the Curriculum*

3.1 *Introduction*

These spelling strategies are for use by pupils of 8+ years. All are suitable for use with primary or secondary pupils. (It is generally assumed that in the secondary school specific attention to spelling will be the responsibility of the English specialist. However, there is of course no reason why the strategies, once taught, should not be adopted across the curriculum.) The information required by pupils is presented in worksheet form, designed for pupils of 10+ years. Teachers of younger children should present the strategies orally, adapting the language and ideas to their pupils' ability level. For pupils of about 10 and over, the pages may be photocopied and given to pupils to read along with the teacher while the strategies are being introduced, then kept for reference.

It is important that any strategy is taught *and retaught* when it is first introduced. Pupils need to become extremely familiar with the routines involved if these are to attain the status of habit.

The strategies may at first seem time-consuming and unwieldy, but as they become habitual the learning of spelling can proceed almost effortlessly. It is therefore worthwhile taking time to drill pupils in the routines for several weeks, to insist on their following them, and to revise each routine occasionally (to pick up stragglers).

A Spelling Record Book

For many of the teaching strategies to be described in this section, it will be necessary to keep a Spelling Record Book for the pupils in your class. This should be an ordinary exercise book with one or two pages devoted to each pupil. Spellings will be added to it when a pupil requests a spelling word (see Section 3.4) and sometimes as part of the marking process (see Section 3.5). The book will gradually become a record of each child's specific spelling difficulties, and therefore the basis for individualised spelling and testing (see Section 3.6).

The record book should be kept in the same place at all times. This should be somewhere where it is readily available to the teacher when pupils come to him/her asking for spellings, and (when possible) when he/she is marking written work.

Pupils should not be able to remove the book to take it to their desks, and for this reason it might be helpful to keep it tied to the teacher's desk!

3.3 *How to learn a spelling word*
(Spelling: Advice to pupils1)

The spelling strategy described on 'Spelling: Advice to pupils 1' is that used in the later books of the *Mind Your Spelling* series. It encourages pupils to process spellings through eye, ear, hand and brain (see Section 1.3), so that whatever each individual pupil's processing strength, he or she has the opportunity to bring it into play while using the strategy.

Pupils whose strength is in visual processing will find that, for them, the most valuable part of the procedure is looking at the words and thinking about the spelling, then writing it from memory and checking back to see if they have spelled it correctly. Those who rely more heavily on auditory processing strategies will benefit particularly from saying the word slowly and clearly, and registering elements of the spelling through auditory channels. However, all pupils should benefit from a multi-sensory approach as they begin to build up their spelling skills. As time goes on, and they become more competent spellers, they will probably refine the strategy to suit more exactly their own needs.

3.4 *'I can't spell this word!'*
(Spelling: Advice to pupils 2)

Instructions for pupils on how to deal with the spelling of words which crop up during their personal writing are given in (Spelling: Advice to pupils 2). This routine should be described carefully to pupils and practised over a few weeks until it becomes second nature. It allows them to develop as fluent writers, unimpeded by concern about spelling at the time of composition, but also to ensure that they have access to correct spellings once composition is complete. At the end of a piece of writing, or during a natural break, the pupil is still involved with the subject matter, so motivation to find the correct spelling persists.

At this point the pupil should bring a list of the spelling words required to the teacher. If any of the words on the list are correctly spelled, they should be ticked and the pupil praised for his/her efforts. Wherever possible teachers should reinforce correct elements of spelling with positive comments. A pupil's confidence is very important to the development of spelling proficiency.

With near misses, the teacher should congratulate the pupil on the correct elements of the word, and then write out the correct spelling on that pupil's page in the Spelling Record Book (see Section 3.2). For totally incorrect spellings, no comment is necessary, but the word should be correctly written out on the pupil's Record Book page.

The teacher should then encourage the pupil to LOOK and THINK, and SAY and LISTEN to the words. The latter involves pronouncing a word slowly and deliberately, splitting it into syllables and attending to vowel sounds. On no account should the pupil spell the word out letter by letter, or split it into individual letter-sounds, as attempts to memorise sequences of alphabet letters or exaggerated letter-sounds impede rapid processing of spelling.

The pupil can then return to his/her place and WRITE the correct spellings into the original text, as corrections. In order to CHECK, he/she should bring the corrected text back to the Spelling Record Book and compare the correction with the teacher's spelling.

No more than three or four spelling words should be given at a time; so if there are more than this, the pupil should be encouraged to deal with his/her corrections in stages. Most pupils can internalise a small number of new spellings at a time, but if too many are given there is a danger of overloading the memory so that the spellings are not learned.

A policy for the marking of spelling errors   **3.5**
(Spelling: Advice to pupils 3)

Teachers spend an enormous amount of time marking or correcting books, and yet their efforts are often in vain. Many pupils, and particularly those who make the most errors, do not benefit significantly from the way their work is marked. It therefore seems sensible to think carefully about one's method of correction and to look for ways of making it productive in terms of pupils' learning.

In the assessment of most written work, spelling is only one element among many. Often teachers will consider that other areas of writing and communication skills are more important than spelling within the context of a particular piece of writing, and in these circumstances attention to spelling will be inappropriate.

In terms of pupils' day-to-day written work, however, it is probably worth picking up the most striking or pervasive of their spelling mistakes, in order that they should not continue making the same errors in the future.

Most teachers realise that there is no point in correcting an undue number of spelling errors in a piece of writing. This can leave pupils' texts awash with red ink, and cause great erosion of confidence. What is more, pupils are unlikely to learn from their corrections if they are confronted with 10 to 15 at once.

As most pupils can easily cope with learning three or four spelling words at a time, four is the maximum number of corrections which should be pointed out on any one piece of work. It might then be possible to ensure that the pupil actually *learns* the correct spellings of up to four words of which he or she was previously unsure. Correct forms of the words selected should be written out clearly at the end of the piece of work, and pupils should be expected to complete these corrections before starting their next piece of writing.

In order to ensure that the correct spellings are learned through the correction process, rather than merely copied out, it is helpful to ask the pupil to write them somewhere other than the page on which the teacher has given the correct form. The pupil should therefore keep a SPELLING PAGE at the back of each of his/her writing books, on which to write out spelling corrections (using the spelling strategy: LOOK and THINK, SAY and LISTEN, WRITE and CHECK) before checking back to the model provided by the teacher.

Writing out corrections is not, however, a motivating task and pupils can sometimes be lax about it, so checking up may become necessary. Teachers can save time on this by using the old monitorial system: appointing a pupil to check that in each book in a pile the corrections have been done, and been done correctly. Books which do not meet the criteria can be referred to the teacher. (As this can have the spin-off effect of doing wonders for the monitor's spelling, it's a good idea to change monitors often so that lots of pupils get a go!)

Again, this is a routine which takes time to establish. In the early stages the teacher has to be firm, and to remind pupils of the stages in the process. After a while, however, it can become established habit, and pupils will gradually gain confidence over the spelling words which cause them particular difficulties.

3.6 Individualised spelling and testing
(Spelling: Advice to pupils 4)

If they follow the strategies outlined so far, your pupils will gradually (over, say, half a term) build up collections of spelling words, which represent their own particular spelling problem areas, on the back pages of their writing books. In addition, the class Spelling Record Book should contain a list of all the words each pupil has asked for over the same period. These are the words each pupil particularly needs to practise – an individualised spelling list tailored to his/her own needs.

You may feel it necessary to add to the list for certain pupils. Before beginning the individualised testing routine, it is worth making a quick spelling review of your pupils' written work, noting in the Spelling Record Book any other words or groups of words you would like particular pupils to practise. For instance, if a pupil has had difficulty with some commonly confused words, and has completed a worksheet to help with these, add them to the list in the form of a short sentence which establishes their correct use, e.g.:

Their books are over there.

He threw the ball through the window.

Which is the wand which the witch gave you?

The pupils' sheet 4 gives instructions to pupils on the collection of spelling words from various books on to one Spelling Page. Once this is done, the books should be collected in. As Sheet 4 says, 'your teacher will arrange' to have the words from the Spelling Record Book transferred into each pupil's list. The transfer of the words can, of course, be done for you by a pupil (choose a good speller!) but the completed lists should be finally vetted by you, to ensure that all spelling on these final SPELLING PAGES is correct before pupils are given time to practise the words.

This final look over each pupil's spelling list also gives you time to make any necessary amendments, e.g. removing words which you think are too difficult for a particular pupil, cutting lists which are far too long, adding to those which should be longer.

Spelling practice from the 'Big Test' can be given as homework or time may be allotted within the classroom, but pupils should be motivated to care about their success. As an aid to motivation the procedure could, occasionally, be used as a Sponsored Spell for fund raising, or the distribution of some coveted privileges (e.g. monitorial positions for the next half term) could depend on it. As all the pupils have lists of words at their own levels and tailored to their needs, all should have a similar chance of success.

Using a dictionary
(Spelling: Advice to pupils 5a and 5b)

3.7

Notes on the use of dictionaries are given in Section 2.4.

The pupils' advice sheets 5a and 5b give basic instructions and practice activities to introduce dictionary use.

Project Spelling Banks (Junior)

3.8

A Project Spelling Bank is easy to organise and very useful.

All that is required is a **blank poster** positioned where it is both easily accessible and easily seen by all pupils.

As the project develops, key words (needed by pupils in their written work) are written on the poster. Print must be large enough to be seen from all over the classroom.

It is particularly helpful if related words can be grouped together, as this also serves as an introduction to the idea of 'word-families'.

Children should be encouraged to consult the poster (LOOK and THINK, SAY and LISTEN, WRITE and CHECK) when they are unsure of spellings in their project writing.

3.9 Specialised vocabulary from subject areas (Secondary)

In each subject area pupils are likely, over the course of a year, to meet a variety of specialised vocabulary, which they are expected to use and spell correctly in their written work. In the early stages of studying a subject, the opportunity to discuss this vocabulary in a language context is a valuable one, not merely from the point of view of spelling, but in the wider area of language awareness.

For this activity, the English teacher would require lists of those 'specialised' words which will be of relevance in particular subject areas over the course of a term. In a first-year Science course involving work on filtration, for instance, the list might include:

experiment	theory
apparatus	filtration
method	liquid
conclusion	(in)soluble
dissolve	evaporate

There would be similar lists for subjects such as Geography, Mathematics, CDT, and so on. They can form the basis of a series of short lessons, looking at word meanings, word-families, structure and spelling.

The improvement in pupils' understanding and spelling as a result of this activity should be adequate motivation for subject specialists to provide lists of prospective new vocabulary at, say, termly intervals. If not, lists can be compiled by reference to a pupil's written work in the same course from a previous year.

It is also useful, however, to ask pupils to compile lists for themselves. A sheet with columns for the various subjects the pupil is taking can be given out in the first week of term, with instructions that the pupil should list all the new or unfamiliar vocabulary that crops up in each subject. Collation of the words on these lists can be enlightening.

How to learn a spelling word

When you have to learn a spelling word, how do you do it? Stare at it? Copy it out a few times? Say the letters to yourself under your breath? And how long do you remember it after you have done that?

The strategy below helps you learn a spelling word as well as possible. If you learn to use it, and follow the routine properly, it will help you to spell using eyes, ears, hand and brain! You should remember the words you learn, and become a better speller.

LOOK at the word.
THINK about it – what must you remember when you're spelling it?

– Tricky bits?

– Double letters?

– Any little words buried in the big word?

– Any silly ways of remembering it?

SAY the word to yourself slowly, breaking it up into syllables.

– And **LISTEN** to the sounds.

– Say the vowels *very* clearly.

It may help to pronounce even the silent letters and syllables (e.g. Wed-nes-day). Try to remember the sounds of the word.

Then **WRITE** the whole word without looking back at it.

CHECK very carefully to see if you've spelled it right.

If yes, *well done*!
If not, start again from the beginning.

Practise this strategy on some spelling words. Make it a habit to use it whenever you are learning the spelling of a new word. Then, after a while, it will become second nature, and you will become a good speller.

'I can't spell this word!'

When you are writing a story or a report, it is silly to waste time worrying about spelling. You should, of course, try to spell as well as you can. But you shouldn't let spelling worries get in the way of what you want to write. Getting your ideas down on paper comes first.

So what do you do when you want to use a word but you're not sure of the spelling? Here is a routine which will help you deal with the problem:

1 Don't stop writing

   *   If you can have a go at the word, do so. Put a faint wiggly line under it, to mark it for later.

   *   If you've really no idea of the spelling, leave a space, so you can come back to the word later.

2 When you have finished your piece of writing, or when you come to a natural break, check back. Find all the words you have missed out or marked (and any others you think you have spelled wrongly).

3 Get a piece of scrap paper and try the words. You might get them right!

4 Then go to check with your teacher. Show him/her your spellings and see if you got any of them right.

5 Your teacher will show you the correct spelling of any words you do not know, by writing them in the Spelling Record Book. Use

to help you learn them.

6 Then go back to your piece of writing and correct your work. If you work in pencil, it should be easy to correct. If you work in pen, cross out errors and write the correct spellings above the words.

7 Check back in the spelling record book to see if they are right.

Do your corrections!

Do-it-yourself correction

Sometimes, you will have time to take a piece of writing through more than one draft. In the early stages, therefore, you need not bother much about spelling at all. You can leave it until you are about to produce the final copy of your work, and then check back over your draft to correct any spelling mistakes.

Often, however, there is no time for more than a single draft of a piece of work. On these occasions, you should read through your work before handing it in, and neatly correct any spelling mistakes you note.

TIPS

- When checking for mistakes, it often helps to read your work aloud (very quietly!), as this slows down your reading and alerts you to things like missed word-endings or missed-out words.

- It can also help to have a piece of scrap paper handy, so that you can try different versions of spellings and decide which is the right one before altering your script

- Watch out for words which are often confused, e.g. *there* and *their* or *to, too* and *two*. Check that you have got the right spelling each time you use these words.

Teacher's corrections

No matter how hard you check, there will be times when you spell words incorrectly. It is up to you to learn from every mistake – make sure you NEVER spell that particular word wrongly again!

1 In each of your writing books, label the back page SPELLING PAGE and use it to build up your collection of corrections.

2 The teacher will write out the correct spellings of some of your misspelled words at the end of each piece of writing.

3 Look carefully at each word and use the spelling strategy to learn it: LOOK and THINK, SAY and LISTEN.

4 When it comes to WRITE and CHECK, use the back SPELLING PAGE to write the word. Don't just copy it – that won't help you learn.

Write the whole word, then check back.

When you have a minute, look back over all the words on your SPELLING PAGE and make sure you know their spellings now. There is no point in spelling a word wrongly more than once!

Tackling your own (and a partner's) spelling black spots

Over the course of a few weeks, your SPELLING PAGES (at the back of writing books) should begin to fill up with words. These words are important for you, because they are the ones you have spelled wrongly at least once. You want to be sure you don't spell them wrongly again.

1   The first stage is to get all these problem words together.

2   Choose whichever of your writing books has the fullest SPELLING PAGE, and add all the words from your other SPELLING PAGES to it.

3   Use this as an opportunity to learn the spelling again.
(LOOK and THINK, SAY and LISTEN, WRITE and CHECK.)

4   There will probably also be some words on your page of the teacher's Spelling Record Book. These are words you were unsure of too. Your teacher will arrange to have them transferred on to your main SPELLING PAGE.

5   Next, take some time to practise the words, until you are sure you know them all.

6   Then comes the Big Test!

7   Work with a partner. You each need a piece of paper and a pencil. Swap SPELLING PAGES, and let your partner test you on your spelling words, then you test your partner on your partner's spelling words. Number the words, so you know you haven't missed any out.

Then mark each other's test papers.

8   If you got any words wrong, practise them again and have another test. These are real black-spot words for you, so you must work hard to make sure you know them.

9   At the end, put your test paper inside your book and hand it to the teacher.

Using a dictionary

When you want to know the spelling of a word, people sometimes say 'Look it up in the dictionary'. This is often easier to say than to do, and it is usually quicker and easier to ask a good speller to write down the word you want. If, however, it isn't possible to ask someone, a dictionary will have to do.

How to use a dictionary

1   You will find words in a dictionary in alphabetical order. Do you know the alphabet? If not, practise it before going on.

2   Think of the alphabet in four quarters:

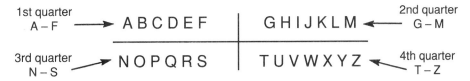

It is easy to work out which quarter the word you want is in. You think of its first letter. Then you can try to open the dictionary at about the right place for that letter.

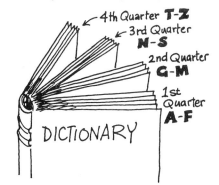

> **PRACTICE ACTIVITY**
> Work with a partner. You each need a dictionary. Choose a letter of the alphabet. When one of you says 'Go', you each try to open your dictionary at the right place for that letter. The one who is nearest is the winner. Have 20 goes and see who wins most.

3   Once you can find the first letter of your word, you have to find the second. Second letters are ordered alphabetically too. Say your word begins with F. Will it be near the beginning of the Fs (like 'fat'), or near the end of the Fs (like 'fun')? Then third letters are ordered alphabetically too. Which comes first: 'fate' or 'family'?

At the top of each page in a dictionary there are two words in **bold print**.

dibble	90	**dim**
dib'ble, *n.* a pointed tool used for making holes for seed or plants. **dice**. See die. **dick'ey**, dick'y, *n.* a back, outside seat of a motor car; a short,		widely spread: containing too many words. **dig**, *v.* to turn up earth or soil (e.g. with a spade): to poke fun or push into (e.g. spurs into a horse).

They are the **key words** for that page.
The left-hand key word tells you what the first word on that page is.
The right-hand key word tells you what the last word on that page is.
Does your word come, alphabetically, somewhere in between them?

Using a dictionary

PRACTICE ACTIVITY

Work with a partner. You each need a dictionary, and paper and pencil. Partner 1 opens the dictionary at any page, writes down the two key words from the top of the page and <u>underlines</u> them.

Then he/she writes a list of ten words starting with the same letter. Four of the words should be words off that page. The other six should be words which are *not* on that page. Mix them up.

dibble – dim
1. drown
2. deed
3. digit
4. dirk
5. dive
6. diet
7. dig
8. devil

Meanwhile, Partner 2 does the same.

When both are finished, swap lists. Tick the four words which would be found on that dictionary page, and cross out the ones which wouldn't. Check with your partner – were you right? Try this activity three times.

4   Once you know how the dictionary is laid out, you should get quicker at finding words.

PRACTICE ACTIVITY

Work with a partner. You each need a dictionary. Choose a word. When one of you says 'Go', you each try to find that word as quickly as you can. The first one to find it is the winner. Try it with five words.

Using a dictionary for spelling

The main problem with looking up spelling words in the dictionary, is that you have got to know more-or-less how to spell them before you can look them up! At least, you've got to know the first few letters. You should therefore always have a go at writing down the spelling on scrap paper before you start. Then you have something to work on.

PRACTICE ACTIVITY

Ask your teacher to give you some difficult spelling words. For each one, try to work out the spelling on scrap paper first, then check it in the dictionary. Can you find it? Was your spelling right?

Section 4: *Helping the poor speller*

What shall I do?

In the average upper primary or lower secondary class, the spelling competence of pupils will vary considerably. Some children seem to pick up and retain spellings effortlessly; others can cope, with a little help and encouragement on a day-to-day basis; some have real difficulties. It is this last group which concerns us here.

The teachers responsible for language work (class teacher in primary school, English teacher in secondary school) have many pressing claims on their time, and helping individual problem-spellers often seems an impossible undertaking. However, many pupils are very severely handicapped by this apparently minor difficulty.

People who cannot spell are often limited in their choice of vocabulary (faced with the apparent impossibility of spelling 'delightful' they will probably opt for 'nice'). They are handicapped in the structure of their prose (while constantly worrying about the spelling of individual words, they lose track of the overall train of thought; so sentence structure and punctuation suffer too). They generally lack confidence about the written word and this shows in the scrappy material they produce (how many reports read 'He/she shows interest in class but has trouble getting it down on paper'?). It also cannot be denied that teachers across the curriculum tend to be adversely affected in their assessment of such pupils' work: poor spelling gives a poor first impression and colours the way a piece of work is interpreted.

It is highly probable that many of these pupils could be helped to attain higher grades in their eventual examination subjects if they could be helped to improve their spelling in the junior/early secondary years, and thus put on course to develop a more confident control of written English.

The following suggestions are based on the assumption that the teacher is anxious to help, but short on time to do so, particularly during class time.

Call in the experts

Spelling difficulties are often associated with reading difficulties and poor spellers should always, in the first instance, be referred to the appropriate authority within a school or area, for a full assessment of reading ability. In some cases this will be a special needs teacher or advisor, in others it may be an educational psychologist. The person concerned should have access to standardised tests of reading, through which the pupil's Reading Age can be established. Other tests can be administered to establish Spelling Age. Many of these tests also give an indication of particular areas of difficulty which are at the root of the pupil's problem.

Where a poor speller is also a poor reader
A child with a reading age which lags more than about 18 months behind his/her chronological age may qualify for special educational needs' provision, appropriate to his/her specific requirements. In this case, the class teacher will be able to liaise with the special needs advisor/teacher who designs the child's learning programme.

Where a poor speller is a good reader
Some poor spellers are good or even above-average readers, but it is still possible that a *specific* language problem exists which is masked by the pupil's overall competency. If possible, therefore, the tester should analyse the pupil's test performance for specific types of error which would give an indication of the cause of the spelling problem.

Teachers are sometimes reluctant to refer pupils for educational tests, but it is a useful way of clarifying a problem and eliciting help in dealing with it in the classroom. The more you know about the problem, the better equipped you are to deal with it. And it may be that help is available of which you were previously unaware.

Further information on help available for children with specific difficulties in spelling may be obtained from:

The British Dyslexia Association
Church Lane
Peppard
Oxfordshire   RG9 5JN
(0734 668271)

The Dyslexia Institute
133 Gresham Road
Staines
Middlesex   TW18 2AJ
(0784 459498)

The Irlen Centre
9 Orme Court
London   W2 4RL
(071 229 8810)

The Dyslexia Information Centre
Hampton Grange
21 Hampton Lane
Solihull   B91 2QJ
(021 705 4547)

Look at the problem

Whether expert help is available or not, a first-hand examination of the pupil's problem by the class teacher is invaluable.

When supervising and marking children's work on a day-to-day basis, teachers do not have time to study errors in depth; nor do they get an overview of a particular pupil's work. It is therefore very illuminating to sit down and examine a wide selection of a particular child's written work in detail. In the case of a poor speller, it is likely that patterns of error will begin to emerge.

Look for evidence of difficulty in the various ways of processing spelling given in Section 1.3. The pointers in the box give an idea of the sorts of things to look for in analysing the pupils' errors.

Problems in spelling by hand

The written work

1 Is handwriting ill-formed, disjointed, immature?

2 Are there many 'impossible' spellings (groups of letters which never go together in English)?

3 Are there frequent perseverations (where a group of letters has been repeated in a word)?

4 Are there frequent b/d reversals?

The pupil

5 Is the pupil poor at drawing and tracing?

6 Does the pupil have problems with left and right?

7 Is he/she left-handed?

8 Has he/she developed odd handwriting habits (e.g. a peculiar pencil grip)?

9 Is he/she cross-dominant (i.e. left-eyed but right-handed, or vice versa)?

A quick check for eye dominance is to see which eye a child chooses when asked to look through a cardboard tube.

Problems in spelling by eye

The written work

1 Are there frequent reversals of words and letters?

2 Are there many 'impossible' spellings (groups of letters which never go together in English)?

3 Are there many 'phonic near-misses' – words where the pupil has obviously used a sound-only approach?

4 Are extremely common irregular words still being misspelled (e.g. was, because)?

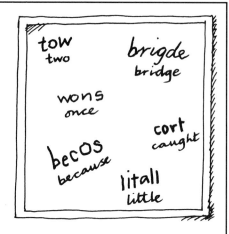

The pupil

5 Did the pupil have difficulty in the earliest stages of reading?

6 Can the pupil reproduce a short sequence of shapes after seeing it for about 30 seconds?
e.g.

7 Does the pupil have problems with left and right?

8 Is he/she left-handed or cross-dominant?

Problems in spelling by ear

The written work

1 Are 'obvious' phonically-regular words misspelled (the sort of word which is easily sounded out)?

2 Are long words often 'telescoped' (syllables missed out, or run into each other)?

3 Are there frequent reversals of words and letters?

4 Does the pupil often omit word endings (e.g. 'ed', 's') and 'little words' (e.g. 'a', 'of', 'to')?

5 Are the letters 'n' and 'm' often omitted in blends (e.g. 'thuder', 'epty')?

The pupil

5 Did the pupil develop any problems with reading after a year or so in school?

6 Has the pupil a history of ear infections/glue ear/hearing problems?

7 Has the pupil also had difficulty in remembering the order of the alphabet, the times tables, etc.?

8 Can the pupil repeat a sequence of letters or numbers which you read out clearly and evenly to him/her? (e.g. A M K T P)

cashed
chased

telosped
telescoped

except
expect

stoakared
shocked

framer
farmer

N.B. It is seldom that a pupil will fit exactly into one category – spelling problems are usually much too complex for that. A poor speller's confidence swiftly deteriorates and this leads to all sorts of errors which are not connected with his/her original problems. The process of analysis is, however, worthwhile in itself, and can lead to the teacher having a much better and more sympathetic grasp of a particular pupil's difficulty. And if errors do seem to fall into one category more than the others, this will be of help in designing strategies and remedial courses.

Call in the pupil

The opportunity for a private interview, at which teacher and pupil can discuss the problem and possible solutions, is invaluable. Most pupils with a spelling problem are only too aware of their handicap and, given the opportunity, are keen to overcome it. The more pupils understand about their problems, and the more they can be involved in planning strategies to deal with them, the more successful such enterprises are likely to be.

Most pupils find that a series of *short* remediation programmes on the problem (with several weeks' break between each one) is more productive than a general, unspecific and potentially infinite approach. To plan a short programme, teacher and pupil need to identify the most glaring problems and draw up a list of aims, which should be relatively easily attainable in the time available. These aims should be clear, specific and reviewed at frequent intervals. Pupils should therefore have a chance to monitor their own progress.

The course of remediation decided upon will, of course, depend very much on the circumstances in each individual case. The author has attempted to draw up general guidelines for pupils in each of the three categories of spelling difficulty described in Section 4.1, and has failed dismally. As in all teaching situations, there is no simple prescription which can be handed out. The teacher and pupil must try to combine awareness of the subject matter (and materials available) with growing awareness of the individual pupil's problem and his/her strengths and weaknesses.

Try to build on strengths, compensate for weaknesses, and if something doesn't work, try something else! The following questions might provide starting points:

1 Is the pupil using all the spelling strategies available to him/her?
   (See Sections 1.3 and 3.3, plus Spelling: Advice to pupils 1)

2 Would the pupil benefit from a structured course through the medium of a workbook (perhaps under parental supervision)?
   (See list of recommended pupil workbooks, page 52)

3 Would the pupil benefit from identifying and clearing up 'backlog errors'?
   (See Section 4.2, Backlog errors 1,2 & 3.)

4   Would the pupil benefit from specific attention to any 'sticky' spelling areas? *(See Section 5.)*

5   Might a short handwriting course be helpful?
    (See The Starter Book of Joined-Up Writing, *Oliver & Boyd, 1990.)*

6   Could a system be devised whereby the pupil proof-reads his/her own written work and has it checked by a good speller before handing it in as completed?
    (See Advice to pupils, Sheet C, and adapt as necessary.)

7   What sort of memory-tricks seems to be particularly helpful to the pupil?

    • Joky mnemonics like 'Never be<u>lie</u>ve a <u>lie</u>'?

    • Alphabetised mnemonics like 'O U Lucky Duck' for the spelling of *could*, *would* and *should*?

    • Exaggerated pronunciation of words like 'def-in-<u>ite</u>-ly'?

    • Auditory mnemonics like 'Wed-NES-day' (all syllables pronounced)?

    • Visual mnemonics like

    • Linking of words with similar letter patterns, e.g. *night, light, might, sight*, etc. and remembering these words as a group?

    • Awareness of linguistic features, such as the *-ly* suffix for adverbs, or the $y \rightarrow i$ *when-adding-an-ending* spelling rule?

Think positively
The capacity to spell accurately is very much bound up with a pupil's self-confidence and self-image. It is therefore particularly important that spelling problems are approached positively and constructively. Negative attitudes to poor spelling will just lead to poorer spelling.

Make sure the pupil knows that:

– Lots of people (including some very clever people) have spelling problems. Einstein, George Washington, Hans Christian Anderson – all were poor spellers. Being a poor speller does not mean you are dim.

– There *is* a system to English spelling, and most words follow the rules and patterns. Don't get down-hearted: BEAT IT!

Give plenty of encouragement, and try to play down any disappointment.

Don't

Don't write, as countless teachers write every day, 'WATCH YOUR SPELLING', 'POOR SPELLING', or 'SPELLING MUST IMPROVE' at the end of each piece of work. Poor spellers are only too aware of their weakness, and need positive help to overcome it, not constant reminders of failure.

Don't try to solve the problem in a week, a month or even a year. Over-ambitious aims lead to loss of confidence, not improvement. Never overface the pupil with work (which, after all, is probably additional to the usual workload of the class). Better to learn three backlog spellings properly than to mess about half-heartedly with ten.

Don't expect instant improvements – most poor spellers have been teaching themselves the wrong spellings and the wrong strategies for many years. It takes a long time to wipe out the errors and change patterns of work.

I don't give a damn for a man that can spell a word only one way.

Mark Twain

4.2 Basic spelling vocabularies and 'backlog errors'

There are certain words which crop up frequently in children's written work and which pupils should therefore be able to spell without effort. When these words can be spelled correctly and effortlessly, pupils are freed to write with more speed and confidence, and the overall appearance of their written work is improved.

Unfortunately, many of these commonly-used words are tricky to spell and children with spelling problems often find them a struggle to learn. All too often they teach themselves an incorrect spelling by constant repetition, and reproduce it for years. These 'backlog errors' contribute to the poor appearance of pupils' work and to their own poor self-image.

It is particularly helpful for poor spellers, therefore, to clear up 'backlog errors' by identifying them and 'overlearning' the correct spelling. Pupils should not be presented with too many such spelling words to tidy up at any one time, and should be offered as much help as possible in terms of learning strategies, mnemonics and repeated checks.

On the next few pages we give several lists at different ability/maturity levels.

Backlog errors 1: The most basic spelling vocabulary
This first list consists of a hundred of the most commonly used words in the English language. Pupils in the early years of the junior school will require to use all these words in their general written work and so should be able to spell them effortlessly. They should be encouraged to write them in joined script, to develop a kinaesthetic image of each word.

Backlog errors 2: Commonly used ...commonly misspelled
This second list consists of approximately 300 further words which are frequently used by writers in upper primary/lower secondary school, but which poor spellers often find tricky. The list is by no means exhaustive; individual pupils will, of course, all have their own particular spelling 'black spots'. It is, however, offered as a starting point. The pupil who can spell all the words listed here effortlessly will find day-to-day writing much less of a problem than the pupil who cannot.

Backlog errors 3: More common errors
The third list has been compiled from errors which commonly occur in the writing of poor spellers in secondary schools (in addition to those given in 'Backlog errors 2'). Again, this is simply a selection of words which have been noted by some teachers as frequently misspelled. It is offered merely as a starting point for pupils and teachers anxious to identify backlog errors which are dogging a pupil's progress.

The most basic spelling vocabulary

a	do	I	on	them
an	did	is	one	there
at	down	in	our	then
as	for	it	out	to
are	from	if	over	today
and	go	into	other	up
all	get	look	old	very
about	give	little	only	we
be	he	like	of	with
but	had	me	off	was
been	have	made	or	were
big	having	make	right	want
before	him	making	so	well
back	his	more	she	went
by	her	must	see	will
can	here	my	said	what
call		much	some	when
come		no	the	where
came		not	that	you
could		now	this	your
coming		new	they	

Commonly used ... commonly misspelled

– se ending

because   'cows attack umbrellas'
house
horse

decide   'I decided to join the C.I.D.
decided

doctor   Exaggerated pronunciation of 'or'
motor
visitor

ex words

next   Useful rule: x is never followed by s in English
extra
example

friend   'I see my friend on Friday.'
                  Friend has end at the end.

field   'My friend fried fish in a field.'

front   Pronounce as in the word 'on'.
month

further   like Thursday and Saturday

do does   Pronounce as: do-es
go goes   go-es

other   like mother and brother
another   (an + other)

across   (a + cross)

work
word
world

after last past ask	These words are not a problem in the north of England. Call them 'Coronation Street' words and pronounce them appropriately.
ask/ed	(ask + ed)
again Brit<u>ai</u>n	Pronounce to rhyme with 'rain'. 'It is r<u>ai</u>ning ag<u>ai</u>n in Brit<u>ai</u>n.
answer people	Pronounce all letters: ans – <u>wer</u> pe + <u>o</u> + ple
before more boring	
any many anything anybody anywhere anyone	(m/any) Learning and practising all these words provides over-learning of the unusual spelling of 'any'.

-ough

br<u>ough</u>t th<u>ough</u>t b<u>ough</u>t f<u>ough</u>t	These words have an Old English spelling. Call them 'O.U.G.H. words' and link them in the pupil's mind by inventing a story containing them all.
en<u>ough</u> r<u>ough</u> t<u>ough</u>	'Are you r<u>ough</u> and t<u>ough</u> en<u>ough</u> to learn the O.U.G.H. words?'
thr<u>ough</u> threw	'The boy threw the ball through the window.'
before behind between because	(be + fore) (be + hind) (be + tween) (be + cause)
ever never every everything everybody everyone everywhere	 (n/ever) (ever + y) (ever/y/thing) (ever/y/body) (ever/y/one) (ever/y/where)

finish(ed)	(fin/ish/ed)	
happen(ed)	(happ/en/ed)	
remember(ed)	(re/mem/ber/ed)	These words provide
yesterday	(yes/ter/day)	opportunites for
probably	(pro/bab/ly)	syllable practice.
holiday	(hol/i/day)	
hospital	(hos/pit/al)	
morning	(morn/ing)	
perhaps	(per/haps)	
animal	(an/im/al)	

high   Old English spelling – call them 'I.G.H. words'.

might   Link to <u>night</u> and <u>fight</u> by making up a story.
right
frightened   (fright/en/ed)

half
walk
talk

just

left
left
soft

found   Pupil can make up a story to link these to other 'ound' words.
round

listen   Pronounce all letters: e.g. 'lis + ten'
often   'I of/ten lis/ten when you fas/ten the gate.'

nobody
nothing
nowhere

minute   'A minute is a minute fraction of a year.'

know   Call this 'k/now', pronouncing the k.
knew

feel
feeling   (feel + ing)
keep
seem

watch   (See sheet 5.12 in Section 5.)
kitchen

hear   'You hear with your ear.'
heard
near
year
nearly
nearby

h<u>ere</u>	'place words'
th<u>ere</u>	
wh<u>ere</u>	
to/too/two	(See sheet 5.4 in Section 5.)
write/right	(See sheet 5.9 in Section 5.)
there/their	(See sheets 5.2 and 5.3 in Section 5.)
could	'<u>O</u> <u>U</u> Lucky <u>D</u>uck'
would	
should	
fire	
tired	
mile	
smile	
while	
young	'You are young.'
use	
used	
used to	
usual	(us/u/al)
self	
selves	
real	
really	(real + ly)
lovely	(love + ly)
beautiful	'<u>B</u>ig <u>E</u>lephants <u>A</u>re <u>U</u>gly.'
	(beau + ti + ful)
awful	
<u>w</u>rong	
<u>w</u>riting	
those	
whose	
w<u>h</u>ose	'wh' saying 'h' instead of 'w'
w<u>h</u>o	
w<u>h</u>ole	

birthday	'The dirty girl got a bird for her first birthday.'
first	
girl	
bird	
dirty	
Britain	
British	
England	Pronounce 'e' as in 'hen'.
English	
pretty	'ET isn't pretty'
question	(ques/ti/on)

happened	(happ/en/ed)	Look for double letters.
supposed	(supp/ose/ed)	
suddenly	(sudd/en/ly)	
appear	(app/ear)	

stopped	(See sheet 5.16 in Section 5.)
stopping	
quick	Link to stick, thick etc.
quickly	
quite/quiet	
white	
write	
together	'We're going to get her together.'
place	Link to race and face.

police	(pol + ice)	'There was a POLICE NOTICE to say it was
notice	(not + ice)	not ice.'

Mr	(Mister)
Mrs	(Mistress/Missus)
maybe	(may + be)
sure	
measure	

picture	(pic + ture - 'ture' like 'sure')
future	(fu + ture)
adventure	(ad + ven + ture)
piece	'A piece of pie.'
paid	
said	
both	
buy	'buy' and 'guy' are the only two 'uy' words
guy	'Buy a guy.'
since	
once	
br<u>ea</u>k	
br<u>ea</u>kfast	explain origin of word
gr<u>ea</u>t	'It's gr<u>ea</u>t to <u>ea</u>t.'
wear	'You w<u>ea</u>r a ring in your <u>ea</u>r.'
h<u>ea</u>rd	'ear' words
<u>ea</u>rly	Link by making up a story.
<u>ea</u>rth	
l<u>ea</u>rn	
s<u>ea</u>rch	
r<u>ea</u>dy	'Ready, steady, go.'
inst<u>ea</u>d	
m<u>ea</u>sure etc.	
m<u>ea</u>n	
m<u>ea</u>nt	
<u>ea</u>sy	
<u>ea</u>ch	
undern<u>ea</u>th	
always	'all' becomes 'al' when used as a prefix
almost	
already	
although	another 'O.U.G.H. word'
altogether	(as in to/get/her)

want what	Either an 'h' or an 'n' - not both; 4 letters only.
went when	Either an 'h' or a 't' - not both; 4 letters only.
couldn't can't doesn't don't wasn't didn't	(See sheet 5.10 in Section 5.)
called	(call + ed)
cold told	(c/old, *etc.*)
<u>war</u>m to<u>war</u>ds for<u>war</u>ds quarter	Use 'war' as the basic spelling for these words. (for + wards)
carry/carrying/carried try/trying/tried lady/ladies baby/babies	(See sheet 5.18 in Section 5.)
caught taught naughty daughter laugh	Another Old English spelling. 'I caught my naughty daughter and taught her not to laugh.'

More common errors

absolute / ly
accept except
accident
  accidental
  accidentally
aloud allowed
among
ancient
appear / ed
  disappear / ed
appoint / ment
  disappoint / ed
area
attempt
  attempted
  (empty)
careful
  powerful
begin
  beginning
believe
build / building
  built
busy / business
care / scare
  parents
  square
centre
  centimetre
  metre litre
  theatre
certain
  certainly
character
circle
colour / ful / ed
  (favourite)
complete / ly
condition
country
  countries
couple

cycle
  bicycle
danger / ous
  (famous,
  enormous)
definite / ly
  (opposite)
delicious
describe
  description
design
develop / ment
different
  (interest / ed)
difficult
direction
during
easy / easily
either / neither
electric
emergency
essential
eventual / ly
  usual / ly
  gradual / ly
  actual / ly
except expect
exciting
  excitement
exercise
experience
experiment
extreme / ly
fair / ly
faithful / ly
family /families
final / ly
foreign
fortunate / ly
  (immediate /ly)
for instance

fourth / fourteen
  (forty)
frequent
fruit
general / ly
government
grateful
growth
guess
heart
heavy / heaven
honest / ly
imagine
  imaginary
important / ance
impossible
improve / ment
including
independent
  independence
inform / ation
leisure
luxury
  luxurious
machine
meanwhile
modern
  (northern,
  southern etc.)
mountain / ous
moving
mustn't
national
natural / ly
necessary
object
obtain
obvious / ly
occasion / al /ly
of course
office (notice,

police, justice)
ought
paragraph
particular / ly
peculiar
period
point
position
possible
  possibly
prepare
probable
  probably
quality
quantity
quarrel / ling
quarter
question
realise
reason
receive
regard
religion
remain
reply / ing
  replied
responsible
  (possible,
  horrible,
  terrible)
rough / ly
satisfy / ing
  satisfied
  satisfactory
secret
  secretary
section
separate
several
sincerely
single

social / society
(e) special / ly
spread
straight
success
  succeed
  (accident)
suit / suitable
suppose
  supposed to
surprise
system
therefore
throughout
touch
true / truth
unknown
valuable
variety
various
vegetable
whatever
wherever
woman
  women
worse / worst

Books for helping deal with spelling problems

Assessment

The following books are very helpful in the assessment of pupils' spelling difficulties:

Essentials in Teaching and Testing Spelling, F J Schonell (Macmillan Education, revised ed. 1985)

Diagnostic and Remedial Spelling Manual, M Peters (Macmillan Education, revised ed.1979)

Workbooks for individual spelling courses

The following expendable workbooks are all designed for use by pupils without a great deal of teacher direction. They may therefore be suitable as the bases of individual structured spelling courses for pupils with spelling problems. All of them are suitable for use with older children.

Teachers may prefer to choose workbooks which will help pupils to build on their existing spelling strategies, or books which will help them develop particular processing skills which they lack. We have therefore also noted the general approaches taken in particular series.

Sounds, Patterns and Words, J Moore (Holmes MacDougall)
> This is a series of four workbooks which takes a phonic approach to spelling, relating groups of words by particular phonic blends.

Catchwords, Charles Cripps (Harcourt Brace Jovanovich)
> The Catchwords series of six workbooks (Blue, Red, Green, Yellow, Orange, Purple) is based on a visual approach to spelling.

Super Spelling Books, Charles Cuff and David Mackay (Longman)
> This series of six workbooks takes an eclectic approach, encouraging visual, auditory and linguistic processing of spelling.

Spell Well, E E Henderson (Blackie)
> Another eclectic series (five books), which begins with a simple phonic approach and later emphasises letter-groups, prefixes, suffixes, etc. It also contains sections on commonly misspelled words.

Read, Write and Spell, Julia Leech and Gillian Nettle (Heinemann)
> A very carefully structured course for pupils with reading/spelling difficulties. It takes a mainly phonic approach, but includes occasional irregular common words which must be learned by non-auditory analysis. Involves more teacher participation than the other workbooks.

Books / material for dyslexic pupils

Alpha to Omega, B Hornsby and F Shear (Heinemann)

This book provides a classic highly-structured course for pupils with specific literacy difficulties, and can be very effective if properly used. However, it really requires one-to-one teaching on a frequent and regular basis. Assuming teacher-time is not available, certain parents (or home-tutors) might be able to use it with their children (given support).

Dealing with Dyslexia, P Heaton and P Winterson (Better Books)

A useful book for parents who wish to use *Alpha to Omega* with their dyslexic children. It gives background information and help in finding a way through the course, as well as other useful material.

Help for Dyslexic Children, T R Miles and Elaine Miles (Methuen)

Again directed at parents and including ideas and material for helping at home. Less detailed and perhaps more manageable for parents than *Alpha to Omega*.

Section 5: *Worksheets on sticking points*

Here is a list of the photocopiable worksheets which follow. These worksheets cover some of the commonest areas of error in English spelling.

Commonly confused words:
5.1   **where** and **were**
5.2   **there** and **their**
5.3   **there**, **their** and **they're**
5.4   **to**, **too** and **two**
5.5   **of** and **off**
5.6   **which** and **witch** (and 'sandwich'!)
5.7   **been** and **being**
5.8   **our** and **are**
5.9   **write/right**, **writing**

Contractions:
5.10   Apostrophe in n't contractions
5.11   Apostrophe in shortened forms (general)

Odds and ends:
5.12   – **tch** words
5.13   – **dge** words
5.14   – **ck** and – **ke** (e.g. snack and snake)
5.15   – **ew** words (including threw/through, knew/new)

Spelling rules:
5.16   Doubling in short verbs
5.17   Dropping final 'e'
5.18   Changing 'y' to 'i' when adding an ending

Help in spelling by ear:
5.19   The short vowel sounds
5.20   Word sums (syllables 1)
5.21   Syllables 2

where and *were*

here, **there** and **where**
These three words are all 'place' words:

Where is my book?
Is it here?
No, it's over there.

were is not related to the three place words. It sounds different (more like 'wur'). It hasn't got an 'h'. It is part of the verb 'to be'.

We were very pleased.
The shops were open.

They all contain the letters: **here**

Copy   here   there   where

Copy we were,   they were
you were

*Fill **were** or **where** into these sentences:*

1   The shops _____ shut.

2   _____ is my ruler?

3   We _____ too late to catch the bus.

4   The trees _____ losing their leaves.

5   How long _____ you asleep?

6   I know a place _____ you can buy cream cakes.

7   I asked _____ she lived.

8   We _____ quite good friends.

9   _____ does your grandmother live?

10 How many people _____ at the party?

_____ are my books?

They _____ on the teacher's desk

Check with your teacher before going on.

11 That's the place _____ I fell off my bike.

12 I know _____ to look for your coat.

13 I wish you _____ living next door!

14 There _____ lots of flowers in the garden.

15 The children _____ playing _____ we had left them.

16 _____ do you think they _____ ?

17 There _____ some marks on the road _____ the accident happened.

18 The books are over there today. _____ _____ they yesterday?

19 I want to know _____ the presents _____ hidden?

20 Why _____ you upset when I asked _____ you had been?

there and *their*

1   **there** is a place word, like 'here' and 'where'. It is also used in these expressions:

there is	there was	there were	there are
_____	_____	_____	_____
there will be	there won't be	there may be	there might be
_____	_____	_____	_____

Copy the six 'there' phrases on the lines underneath.

2   **their** is a pronoun. It means 'belonging to them' (like 'our' means 'belonging to us').

their books	their names	their football	their house
_____	_____	_____	_____

Copy the four 'their' phrases on the lines underneath.

BOTH WORDS BEGIN WITH **THE**

3   *Choose the correct word – **there** or **their** – and fill in the spaces.*

    a) Put it over _____ .

    b) They left _____ gloves in the cloakroom.

    c) Once upon a time _____ were three bears.

    d) _____ is a fly in my soup!

    e) The boys lost _____ way.

    f) I don't know the way _____ .

    g) How many people were _____ at the party?

    h) Is it yours? No it's _____ s.

    i) Are _____ many pages left to read?

    j) I think _____ might be a good film on television.

Check with your teacher before going on.

    k) The people weren't sure of _____ way.

    l) I left them at _____ house.

    m) The children enjoyed _____ lunch.

    n) Where is it? It's _____ .

    o) We looked here, _____ and everywhere, but we couldn't find _____ sandwiches.

    p) I hope _____ are some bears at the zoo.

    q) Put _____ coats and hats over _____ .

ZOO

there, their and *they're*

(all begin with **the**)

there	**the**ir	**the**y're
a place word	a possessive pronoun (belonging to them)	Short for 'they are'

Here and **there**. **There** is	They put **their** books in **their** schoolbags.	**They're** singing carols. **They're** not ready.

*Choose the correct word – **there**, **their** or **they're** – to fill in each space.*

1 _____ all very excited about Christmas.

2 _____ are 50 pages in my book.

3 Where should the children leave _____ coats and hats?

4 We left our coats over _____.

5 I'm visiting my cousins. I hope _____ at home when I arrive.

<u>*Check with your teacher before going on.*</u>

6 I was late setting off for school, but I got _____ just in time.

7 _____ too tired to come out this afternoon.

8 They put _____ names at the top of _____ papers.

9 Are _____ many people in the waiting room?

10 _____ are four men waiting, but _____ wives have gone home.

11 The dogs got _____ paws wet in the river.

12 The boys enjoy cricket, but _____ not very good at football.

13 Here are my sums. I'm afraid _____ all wrong.

14 The children wanted to have _____ party outside.

15 Is _____ a doctor in the house?

*Make up three sentences of your own, containing the words **there**, **their** and **they're**.*

_____

_____

_____

Spelling *A Teacher's Survival Kit*   © *Oliver & Boyd 1991*

to, two and *too*

to = a little word which is very common

two = 2

too = 'more than enough'
too = 'as well' } two meanings

*Fill **to**, **too** or **two** into these sentences:*

1   The little boy was _____ years old last Friday.

2   My friend went _____ France for her holidays.

3   The water is _____ cold for swimming.

4   Do you know the way _____ our school?

5   The teacher looked as if he was going _____ explode.

6   She wore the same socks for _____ days.

7   I'd like some potatoes, please. And I'll have some peas _____.

8   It's _____ late for a story. Go straight _____ sleep.

9   At _____ o'clock we are going _____ the shops.

10 The tea was _____ hot _____ drink.

Check with your teacher before going on.

11 There were _____ birds sitting in a tree.

12 My sister is _____ young _____ join the Brownies.

13 I am going _____ watch TV for _____ hours.

14 Don't forget _____ put your coat on. And please bring my coat _____.

15 _____ girls on one chair is one _____ many.

The two meanings of 'too'

In the little story below, 'too' is used eight times. Wherever it means 'more than enough', underline it (five times). Wherever it means 'also', put a (ring) round it (three times).

There were too many people in the little car. There were too many pets in there too. Bess the sheepdog was too big to sit down in the boot and her puppy was too wriggly to sit on Mrs Brown's knee. The Brown family were too hot and sticky to enjoy their ride, and the animals were miserable too.
'I wish I'd stayed at home,' said Sarah Brown.
'Me too,' said her brother.

of and *off*

sounds like 'ov'

The Prince *of* Wales.
A bunch *of* flowers.

sounds like 'off'

On and *off*.
Take *off* your shoes.

*Fill the correct word – **of** or **off** – into each space:*

1 The King _____ Spain's daughter came to visit me.

2 The clock fell _____ the shelf and landed on the cat.

3 We are _____ to sunny Spain.

4 There are lots _____ boys called James.

5 A pair _____ robins have made a nest in our garage.

Check with your teacher before going on.

6 The gun went _____ by mistake.

7 My cards were the three _____ clubs and the ace _____ hearts.

8 Switch _____ the kettle and make a cup _____ tea.

9 As I was getting _____ the bus, I saw some _____ my friends.

10 Plenty _____ children have time _____ school.

11 Take _____ your coat and sit down.

12 _____we go!

13 They had to put _____ the girl's birthday party because she was ill.

14 One _____ the kittens was black and white.

15 I looked out _____ the window and saw Fred fall _____ his bike.

*Make up two sentences of your own containing the word **of**, and two sentences containing the word **off**. Write the sentences here and <u>underline</u> the words **of** or **off** in each one.*

_____

_____

_____

_____

Spelling *A Teacher's Survival Kit*   © *Oliver & Boyd 1991*

which and *witch* (and 'sandwich'!)

A lot of question words start with **wh**:

Copy: what   where   why   when   which   who

Use each word in a question sentence:
What are you doing ?

_____

_____

_____

_____

Which is one of these questioning words. It can also be used to refer back to

something, e.g. The box which I left on the shelf.

The dog which ate the sausages.

Fill which into these sentences, and draw an arrow to show what it is referring back to in each case:

1   I gave him the sword _____ the king had given me.

2   She tried on the shoes _____ she had bought earlier.

3   The door _____ led to the kitchen was closed.

4   Here are the cakes _____ we kept for you.

On the other hand, a lady with a tall black hat is a 'witch'.
She has a 't' in the middle and no 'h' near the beginning.

*Put **which** or **witch** into these sentences:*

5   _____ coat is yours?   6   The _____ cast a spell.

7   The cat belonged to a _____ .

8   _____ is the best way home?

9   She asked me _____ was _____.

10 _____ _____ won the Supernatural Beauty Contest?

11 I wonder _____ is the right answer.

12 Tell me _____ of the books you prefer.

13 This is the car _____ won the race.

14 The farm, _____ was a large one, was along the road.

sandwich

Which has got an **h**. **Witch** has got a **t**. But **sandwich** hasn't got either.
Complete:

This is the sand_____ _____ the _____ made for her tea.

been and *being*

been follows the verb 'to have', e.g. have, has, having, had.

being follows the verb 'to be', e.g. is, was, am, are, were. Or it can stand alone.

*Put **been** or **being** into these sentences:*

1   Have you _____ to school today?

2   We are _____ tested on our spelling today.

3   The boy was _____ given a hard time by his friends.

4   He has _____ reading that book all morning.

5   The teachers have _____ going on at us all day.

6   Where has that dog _____?

7   You are _____ very kind to me.

8   Nobody asked whether he had _____ to see me.

9   _____ tidy can take up quite a lot of your time.

10 Having _____ to London, she knew a lot about its history.

11 _____ English, she wasn't sure how to pronounce French words.

12 Are you _____ served?

13 Have the other children _____ nice to you?

14 There is no way of _____ friendly to a savage dog.

When shortened forms of words are used, you have to think what they are short for.

1   I've _____ up to London to visit the Queen. (I have)

2   They're _____ very unkind to their uncle. (They are)

3   We're _____ as careful as we can.

4   You've _____ to the sweet shop, haven't you?

5   Where's she _____ ?

6   It's _____ a long time since we met.

7   Who's _____ sitting in my chair?

our and *are*

THIS IS OUR HOUSE

WHERE ARE YOU?

our means 'belonging to us'.
It is a pronoun (like your).

are is part of the verb 'to be' (like is).

Complete:

____ house, ____ street, ____ town. We ____, ____ you, they ____.

____ coats, ____ shoes, ____ socks. Here ____, there ____, where ____?

____ hands, ____ heads, ____ brains. Who ____, what ____, why ____?

*Fill **our** or **are** into the spaces:*

1 Where _____ the children playing?

2 We put _____ sandwiches in the box.

3 _____ teacher is called Mr Singh.

4 There _____ lots of flowers in the park.

5 We called _____ dog Tramp because he was so scruffy.

6 The police _____ searching the building.

7 How many people _____ in there?

8 You can put your car in _____ garage for now.

9 We don't know where they _____ .

10 We gave _____ names to the man at the door.

11 Your books _____ over there, but I don't know where ____ s ____.

12 _____ Father, which art in Heaven.

13 There _____ strangers at front door.

14 We left _____ coats in the cloakroom and now they _____ missing.

write and *right* (and *'writing'*)

You can **write** a letter.   You can get your sums **right**.   You can turn **right** or left.

This 'write' has a silent 'w' at the beginning. It is a verb.

This 'right' has a silent 'gh' in the middle.

You *either* have a silent 'w' **or** a silent 'gh'. You don't have both!

Copy: You can write a letter.

Copy: Put up your right hand if you get it right.

*Choose the correct spelling – **write** or **right** – to fill in each of these blanks:*

1 I got all the answers _____ .

2 We are going to _____ a story this afternoon.

3 Do you know the _____ way to do this?

4 I can't remember which is my _____ hand, and which is my left.

5 Turn _____ at the end of the road.

6 _____ your name at the top of this sheet.

7 That's _____ . You can _____ very neatly.

8 Most people _____ with their _____ hands.

9 We had to _____ down the _____ answers to the questions.

10 The dog bit _____ to the bone.

Write + ing = writing. *Fill **write** or **writing** into the blanks:*

1 Can you join up your _____ ?

2 I like _____ poems, but it takes ages to _____ a good one.

3 Your _____ is very good, but don't _____ in the margin.

Apostrophe in n't contractions

n't is short for 'not'.
The apostrophe (') shows where the letter 'o' has been missed out.
You do not need to add or miss out any other letters.

1   *Fill in the missing words, as shown in the first example. When you have finished, cover your writing up with card or paper, and spell the **n't** forms from memory in the last column.*

COVER AND CHECK

was + not	= was not	= wasn't	_____
are + not	= _____	= _____	_____
do + not	= _____	= _____	_____
could + not	= _____	= _____	_____
should + not	= _____	= _____	_____
would + not	= _____	= _____	_____
were + not	= _____	= _____	_____
have + not	= _____	= _____	_____
had + not	= _____	= _____	_____
is + not	= _____	= _____	_____
did + not	= _____	= _____	_____
has + not	= _____	= _____	_____
does + not	= _____	= _____	_____
must + not	= _____	= _____	_____

2   Two strange ones. *Copy them underneath:*

can + not   =   cannot   =   can't   will + not   =   will not   =   won't

_____   =   _____   =   ____   _____   =   _____   =   _____

3   *Find 8 (**+ not**) words in this passage, cross them out and write the short **n't** form over the top.*

can't
I ~~cannot~~ understand why he did not come to the party. I could not have forgotten to post his invitation. Perhaps he was not well, or his parents were not there to give him a lift. Perhaps he had not made a note of the time, or he does not check his diary often enough. Anyway, he did not ring up to apologise and he has not been in touch. Perhaps I should not have bothered to ask him.

Apostrophe in shortened forms

An apostrophe looks like a flying comma ('). You can use it to show that you have missed some letters out of a word or words. We use it most often when two words are squashed together so that some letters disappear.

For example: it is ➜ it's
                I have ➜ I've

THE APOSTROPHE GOES WHERE THE LETTERS HAVE BEEN MISSED OUT

1   *Write the complete version of these shortened forms:*

I'm = _____   you're = _____   he's = _____   she's = _____

we're = _____   they're = _____   I'll = _____   you'll = _____

I've = _____   you've = _____   they've = _____

I should've = _____   you would've = _____

he could've = _____   they might've = _____

2   *Write the shortened forms of these groups of words:*

we have = _____   you should have = _____

I had = _____   we would = _____

they will = _____   she had = _____

you are = _____   they are = _____

they had = _____   we shall = _____

let us = _____   what is = _____

who is = _____   there is = _____

of the clock = ___   Hallow even = _____

3   The word 'not' is often shortened to 'n't'. The rest of the spelling doesn't usually change.

Write the shortened forms of these groups of words:

could not = _____   have not = _____

is not = _____   would not = _____

does not = _____   had not = _____

must not = _____   cannot = _____

-tch words

1 Complete these **-tch** words:

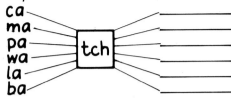

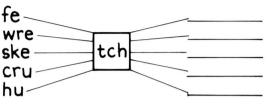

2 Now select the right **-tch** word for these clues:

a) used for telling the time = _____

b) bring = _____

c) found on a door = _____

d) piece of material = _____

e) used to light a fire = _____

f) a group = _____

g) a rough drawing = _____

h) grab (out of the air) = _____

i) used to help a lame person = _____

j) poor soul = _____

k) home for a rabbit = _____

3 Complete these **-tch** words:

bi
di
pi
wi
sti
swi

tch

4 Make up clues and write answers for the **-tch** words:
For example: female dog = bitch

1 _____ = _____

2 _____ = _____

3 _____ = _____

4 _____ = _____

5 _____ = _____

6 _____ = _____

7 _____ = _____

5 Fill suitable **-tch** words into the gaps so that these sentences make sense:

1 The wicked _____ fell in a _____ .

2 If you can't _____ the ball you had better _____ instead.

3 _____ on the light and put the _____ down on the door.

4 We shall go to see the _____ at the football _____ .

5 I like to _____ television.

-dge words

-dge is found at the ends of words.

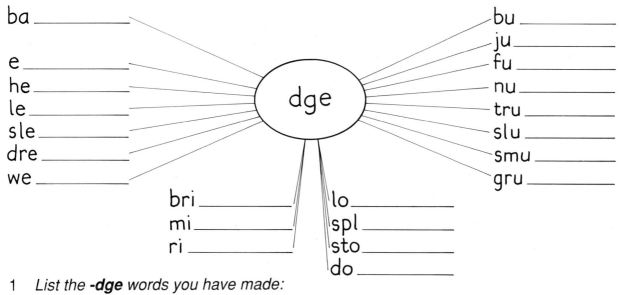

ba _____

e _____

he _____

le _____

sle _____

dre _____

we _____

dge

bu _____

ju _____

fu _____

nu _____

tru _____

slu _____

smu _____

gru _____

bri _____

mi _____

ri _____

lo _____

spl _____

sto _____

do _____

1   List the **-dge** words you have made:

_____ _____ _____ _____

_____ _____ _____ _____

_____ _____ _____ _____

_____ _____ _____ _____

2   Fill the most suitable **-dge** words into these gaps:

a) The flowers were on the window - _____ .

b) The _____ said the prisoner could leave the court.

c) We had great fun in the snow playing with the _____ .

d) Mum cut a large _____ of cake.

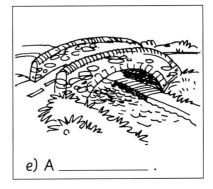

e) A _____ .

3   Find four more words containing **-dge** to answer these clues:

a) black and white British animal = b _____

b) a very small person = m _____

c) brightly-coloured bird, often kept as a pet = b _____

d) someone who lives as a 'paying guest' in someone else's home = l _____

4   Turn this sheet over and, without looking back, write down as many **-dge** words as you can remember.

-*ck* and -*ke*

peck   crack
black   (ck follows a short vowel sound ă ĕ ĭ ŏ ŭ)   luck
neck   clock
lock   thick
stick   duck

make
hike   (ke follows a long vowel sound ā ē ī ō ū)   smoke
spoke   duke
bike   lake
Peke   like

1   *Add* -**ck** *or* -**ke** *to complete the words:*

| I li __ my friend | The Du _ _ of Wellington | A poisonous sna _ _ |
| I li __ my friend | The du _ _ of Wellington | A poisonous sna _ _ |

2   *Add* -**ck** *or* -**ke** *to make ten English words:*

sma _ _   spo _ _ n   qui _ _ ly   stu _ _   bi _ _

bro _ _ n   stri _ _   bra _ _ s   earthqua _ _   thi _ _

lu _ _ y   flo _ _   milksha _ _   bla _ _ board keepsa _ _

When we add +**ing**, we take the **e** off **ke** words:

like ➜ liking
But **ck** words keep both their letters:

lick ➜ licking

3   The unfinished words in these sentences can be completed by adding either **-cking** or **-king**. *Complete the words correctly:*

a) The sign said NO SMO _____ .   NO SMO

b) Grandma was in the kitchen ba _____ a cake.

c) Mum was ba _____ the car out of the garage.

d) We were sti _____ stamps on the envelopes for two hours.

e) We are going on a hi _____ holiday in Wales.

f) I have taken a li _____ to raspberry yoghurts.

g) That dog is li _____ something disgusting off the pavement.

Please note these **-ken** words:

spoken ta _____ wo _____ wa _____ bro _____ forsa _____

-ew words

ow → ew

bl_____
gr_____
thr_____
kn_____

(ow)

_____
_____
_____
_____

bl_____
gr_____
thr_____
kn_____

(ew)

_____
_____
_____
_____

present = bl**o**w   past = bl**e**w

1   *Fill **blow** or **blew** into these sentences:*

   a)   Today I _____ my nose. Yesterday I _____ my nose.

   b)   Last week the roses _____ two inches. This week I hope they will _____ another inch.

   c)   Do you _____ your date of birth? My brother _____ his date of birth when he was two.

   d)   Last Monday, Javid _____ the javelin in the school sports. Today he is going to _____ it again.

threw and through

He **threw** the ball **through** the window.

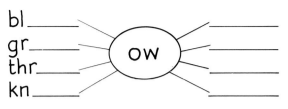

2   *Fill **threw** or **through** into these sentences:*

   a)   The train went _____ the tunnel.

   b)   I _____ a six.

   c)   Who _____ that stone?

   d)   We look all _____ the book and couldn't find the picture.

knew and new

She **knew** that it was a **new** hat.

3   *Fill **knew** or **new** into these sentences:*

   a)   I never _____ his name.   b)   Is that your _____ coat?

   c)   The _____ car goes like a bomb.   d)   You _____ the way.

   e)   Happy _____ Year!   f)   The dog _____ the way home.

4   *Cover up the top of the page and fill in the spaces below:*

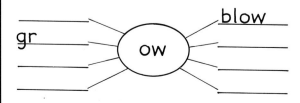

gr_____

blow
_____
_____
_____

(ow)

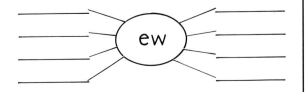

(ew)

_____
_____
_____
_____

Doubling letters in short verbs

You sometimes have to double the final letter of a verb when you add an ending such as – **ed** or – **ing**.

single vowel
tap
single consonant

single vowel
rub
single consonant

You need to double if the verb is a
one-syllable word ending in a single vowel + a **single** consonant
e.g. tap   get   sit   stop   rub.

(N.B. The vowels are a, e, i, o, u and the consonants are all the other letters.)

1   *Add -ing to these words, doubling the final letter where necessary:*

rub rubbing	snip _____	lick _____	sail sailing
drag _____	stub _____	knit _____	loop _____
foam _____	swim _____	weep _____	flit _____
boil _____	whip _____	float _____	hop _____
pat _____	wait _____	shop _____	walk _____
hug _____	fold _____	wheel _____	trip _____
hold _____	kneel _____	wail _____	ring _____
step _____	bet _____	grab _____	clap _____
slim _____	rip _____	flip _____	fail _____
stoop _____	keep _____	shoot _____	slip _____
steep _____	tug _____		

Ask you teacher to mark your paper so far, to see that you have got the idea.
Discuss any mistakes.

2   *Now try these:*

fool _____	roam _____	clip _____	clip _____
slam _____	sob _____	tell _____	leap _____
sell _____	bawl _____	snip _____	trim _____
spot _____	fight _____	quack _____	stick _____
drop _____	bid _____	wrap _____	stop _____
get _____			

Dropping final 'e'

The following rule will **usually** work. Unfortunately, English being English, there are a few exceptions, but we won't bother with them here.

hop e

> You drop final (silent) 'e' if you add an ending **beginning with a vowel** (or y),
> e.g. –ing – ive – ous – able – er – ed – ant – al –y.

1   *Complete these words:*

hope + ing = ___hoping___

come + ing = _____

love + ing = _____

have + ing = _____

expense + ive = _____

relate + ive = _____

love + able = _____

like + able = _____

excite + able = _____

fame + ous = _____

adventure + ous = _____

excite + ing = _____

surprise + ing = _____

decide + ing = _____

use + ing = _____

care + ed = _____

live + ed = _____

refuse + al = _____

arrive + al = _____

fine + al = _____

ice + y = _____

shine = y = _____

noise + y = _____

> You DON'T drop final (silent) 'e' when the ending **begins with a consonant**,
> e.g. – ly – ful – less – ty – ment.

2   love + ly = ___lovely___

lone + ly = _____

safe + ly = _____

late + ly = _____

live + ly = _____

like + ly = _____

safe + ty = _____

hate + ful = _____

care + ful = _____

care + less = _____

hope + less = _____

pave + ment = _____

Changing 'y' to 'i' when adding an ending

The letter 'y' can be used to make an 'i' sound at the end of words.
It can be a 'short i', as in happy,
or a 'long ī' as in try.
When you add an ending to these words, you usually change the 'y' to 'i'
e.g. happiness, happily, tries, tried.

1   In the box, there are some word endings. Use them to make as many new words as you can from each of the words in the chart below. Change the 'y' to 'i' and add endings from the box:

ly	er	est	ful
ed	es	ness	

happy	happily happier happiest happiness
easy	
spooky	
beauty	
heavy	
dusty	
pretty	
cry	
supply	
carry	
busy	
reply	
hurry	

N.B.
The rule does not apply when 'y' is used to make the end sound <u>along with a vowel</u>

e.g. sta<u>y</u>, ke<u>y</u>, enjo<u>y</u>, bu<u>y</u>,

sta<u>y</u>ed, ke<u>y</u>s, enjo<u>y</u>s, bu<u>y</u>er.

There is one main exception to the rule. You do not change the **y** to **i** when the ending begins with 'i'.

(If you did you'd have two 'i's together, and that would look silly.)

e.g. marry ➜ marrying   try ➜ trying   reply ➜ replying

2   Add **-ing** to these words:

cry _____   supply _____   carry _____

fly _____   apply _____   hurry _____

The short vowel sounds

1   There are five vowels: **a, e, i, o, u**. Each one of them can make many different sounds. The most common sound a vowel can make is its *short vowel* sound. Listen to the *short vowels* in these words:

păt	pĕt	pĭt	pŏt	pŭt

The ˘ mark shows a short vowel.

Which of the words from the box goes with each of these?

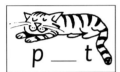 p __ t    p __ t    p __ t

A deep hole – p __ t   To place – p __ t

2   *Fill in vowels to make words. All the vowels will have a short vowel sound. (Only real words are allowed.)*

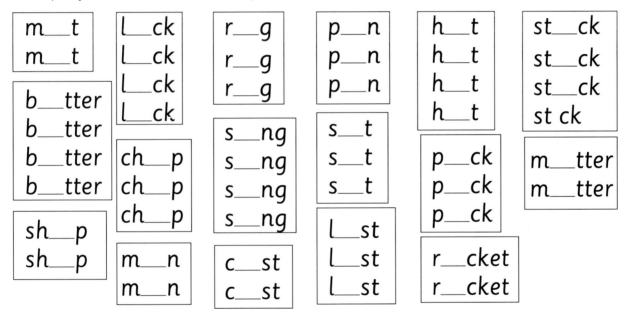

3   Find some more groups of words like the ones in 2. Each group should have the same spelling except for the *vowel*. The vowels should all be *short vowels*. Write your groups of words on the back of this sheet. (N.B. Three-letter words are best.)

4   *Fill in the missing vowels to make these sentences make sense. (They are all short vowels: ă, ĕ, ĭ, ŏ, ŭ.)*

a)   We p__t the sweets in our p__ckets.

b)   My h__bby __s st__mp c__ll__ct__ng.

c)   My jeans are made of d__n__m.

d)   The m__n w__nt to the sh__ps to g__t food.

e)   The c__t c__t __ts l__g __n __ b__t of gl__ss.

Word sums (syllables 1)

Long words are built up out of smaller bits, called **syllables**. You can build a word up from its syllables as if it were a sum.

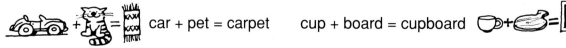 car + pet = carpet   cup + board = cupboard

1   *Fill in the missing parts of these* **word sums**:

cap + tain = _____   pic + ture = _____   per + mit = _____

cur + tain = _____   ____ + ture = future   ____ + son = person

____ + tain = mountain   tor + ____ = torture   per + form = perform

Bri + ____ = Britain   mix + ture = _____   per + haps = _____

cer + tain = _____   ____ + ture = creature   ____ + fect = perfect

2   *Fill in the missing syllables –* **tain**, **ture**, **per** *– to make English words:*

tor ____   ____ haps   moun ____   ____ fume

foun ____   pas ____   ____ mission   adven ____

3   The following words have three syllables each.
    Fill in the missing parts of the word sums:

per + form + er = _____   vol + can + o = _____

in + form + er = _____   tor + _____ + o = torpedo

____ + port + er = reporter   pot + at + o = _____

ex + ____ + er = exporter   tom + ____ + ____ = tomato

4   Every syllable in an English word has at least one vowel: **a   e   i   o   u***

Write out all the groups of words we have made on this page, divide them into syllables, and underline the vowels. The examples will show you how:

cap/tain   pic/ture   per/mit   per/for/mer   vol/can/o

_____   _____   _____   _____   _____

_____   _____   _____   _____   _____

_____   _____   _____   _____   _____

_____   _____   _____   _____   _____

* ('y' can also count as a vowel when it is making an 'i' sound)

Syllables 2

When you are spelling long words, it helps to break them up into smaller bits called syllables.

su / per / cal / i / frag / i / lis / tic (8) = supercalifragilistic

1   *Fill in the missing words or syllables, and write the correct number of syllables in the brackets after each word:*

sta / tion = station (2)	add / i / tion = _____ ( )
na / tion = _____ ( )	___ / tion = fraction ( )
des / tin / a / tion = _____ ( )	___ /__ / tion = subtraction ( )
in /___ / a /___ = information ( )	___ / _ /___ /_ /___ = multiplication ( )
_ / am /_/ a /___ = examination ( )	_ /___ /_ /___ = invitation ( )
_ / ___ /_ / ___ = explanation ( )	___ /___/ _ /___ = distribution ( )

2   Every syllable has at least one vowel (or the letter y, saying 'i')

h<u>a</u>p / p<u>y</u>   d<u>i</u>s / tr<u>i</u>b / <u>u</u> / t<u>io</u>n   b<u>i</u> / c<u>y</u>c / l<u>e</u>

Underline the vowels in the syllables marked in 1.

3   A common final syllable is **-le**.
   a) *Fill in the missing words or syllables.*
   b) *Write the number of syllables in the brackets after the word.*
   c) *Find at least one vowel in each syllable and underline the vowels.*

tab / le = _____ (2)	poss / ib / le = possible ( )
bi /___ / le = bicycle ( )	_ /___ / _ /__ = impossible ( )
___ / _ / ab /_ = vegetable ( )	___ / ib / _ = sensible ( )
___ /___ /_ /_ = comfortable ( )	re /___ /_ / _ = responsible ( )
___ / er /_ /_ = miserable ( )	___ / _ / _ = horrible ( )
___ / ___ / _ = probable ( )	___ / _ / le = terrible ( )

4   *Finish these sentences by writing suitable words in the spaces. All the spaces can be filled by words we have practised in* 1 *and* 3 *above.*

a)   The _____ sums were _____ .

b)   I rode my _____ to meet the train at the _____ .

c)   I got an _____ to a party but I have got to sit an _____ on that day.

d)   I felt _____ because I was _____ for the accident.

Selected Bibliography

BENTLEY, D and KARAVIS, S, *Bright Ideas: Spelling* (Scholastic, 1987)

BRYANT, P and BRADLEY, L, *Children's Reading Problems* (Blackwell, 1985)

CLAY, M, *The Early Detection of Reading Difficulties* (Heinemann, 1979)

D E S / W O, *English in the National Curriculum* (HMSO, 1990)

DONALDSON, M, *Sense and Sensibility: Some Thoughts On The Teaching Of Literacy* (Centre for the Teaching of Reading, Reading University, 1989)

DUNSBEE, T and FORD, T, *Mark My Words* (NATE, 1980)

GENTRY, J R, *SPEL is a Four-Letter Word* (Scholastic, 1987)

H M I, *The Teaching and Learning of Reading in Primary Schools* (DES, 1991)

MILES, T R, *Dyslexia – The Pattern of Difficulties* (Granada, 1983)

MONAGHAN, R and PALMER, S, *Words Alive* (Oliver & Boyd 1989)

MORRIS, J, *A Future for Phonics 44* in *Primary English in the National Curriculum* ed. Huntercarsch, Beverton and Dennis (Blackwell, 1990)

NICHOLS, R, *Helping Your Child To Spell* (Centre for the Teaching of Reading, Reading University, undated)

PETERS, M L, *Spelling: Caught or Taught? A New Look* (Routledge & Kegan Paul, 1983)

PETERS, M L, *Diagnostic and Remedial Spelling Manual* (Macmillan Educational, revised 1979)

REASON, R and BOOTE, R, *Learning Difficulties in Reading and Writing* (NFER-Nelson, 1986)

REID, J and DONALDSON, M, *Letterlinks* (Holmes McDougall, 1988)

SCHONELL, F, *Essentials in Teaching and Testing Spelling* (Macmillan Educational, revised 1985)

S E D, *English Language 5 – 14* (Curriculum & Assessment in Scotland Working Paper No. 2, 1990)

TORBE, M, *Teaching Spelling* (Ward Lock Educational, 1977)

UNDERWOOD, G and UNDERWOOD, J, *Cognitive Processes in Reading and Spelling in Literacy* ed. Cashdan (Blackwell, 1986)

WENDON, L, *First Steps in Letterland / Big Strides in Letterland* (Letterland Ltd, 1986)